NOW YOU KNOW

NOW YOU KNOW

The Book of Answers

Doug Lennox

THE DUNDURN GROUP
TORONTO · OXFORD

Publisher: Anthony Hawke
Editor: Jennifer Bergeron
Illustrations: Catriona Wight
Design: Jennifer Scott
Printer: Transcontinental

National Library of Canada Cataloguing in Publication Data

Lennox, Doug
Now you know : the book of answers/Doug Lennox.

Includes index.
ISBN 1-55002-461-2

1. Questions and answers. I. Title.

AG195.L45 2003   031.02   C2003-903531-X

3   4   5   07   06   05   04   03

Canadä

We acknowledge the support of the **Canada Council for the Arts** and the **Ontario Arts Council** for our publishing program. We also acknowledge the financial support of the **Government of Canada** through the **Book Publishing Industry Development Program** and **The Association for the Export of Canadian Books**, and the **Government of Ontario** through the **Ontario Book Publishers Tax Credit** program, and the **Ontario Media Development Corporation**'s **Ontario Book Initiative.**

Care has been taken to trace the ownership of copyright material used in this book. The author and the publisher welcome any information enabling them to rectify any references or credit in subsequent editions.

J. Kirk Howard, President

Printed and bound in Canada.✪
Printed on recycled paper.
www.dundurn.com

Dundurn Press	Dundurn Press	Dundurn Press
8 Market Street	73 Lime Walk	2250 Military Road
Suite 200	Headington, Oxford,	Tonawanda NY
Toronto, Ontario, Canada	England	U.S.A. 14150
M5E 1M6	OX3 7AD	

This book is dedicated to
Heidi and Hunter

ACKNOWLEDGEMENTS

wish to acknowledge the support of Jean-Marie Heimrath and Dawn Schultz. Their help was immeasurable.

CONTENTS

INTRODUCTION

This book is a collection of scripts originally written for radio and first heard on Sound Source Network's syndicated radio show, "Now You Know."

The concept was born while I was producing another Standard Broadcasting series, "Life in the Twentieth Century." During the mixing, my technical wizard, Gary Mottola, would invariably react to scripted anecdotal information with, "I didn't know that," to which I would respond, "Well, now you know." That repeated exchange started me thinking along a different track that led to this project.

The DNA of a culture is found within its language and rituals. These are our living links to the past. Without realizing it, hundreds of times each day we express the thoughts and ideas of our ancestors through our words and customs. The custom of two people shaking hands upon meeting comes from a Roman practice, for example, and the expression "sleep tight" dates back to the sixteenth century.

The scripts that comprise this book, although thoroughly researched, are not academic studies, but rather, they are meant to entertain and arouse curiosity. Originally confined to thirty-second radio blurbs, the information within is concise, eclectic, and often fascinating. You'll learn how history is alive within each of us and in fact woven into the routines of our everyday existence.

Just enjoy it!

Doug Lennox
Toronto, May 2003

PEOPLE & PLACES

Why do we call New York the "The Big Apple?"

During the 1940s, Robert Emmerich, who played piano in the Tommy Dorsey Band, wrote an obscure song called "The Big Apple." It was soon forgotten by everyone except legendary reporter Walter Winchell, who liked the song so much that in his daily column and on the air he began referring to his beat, New York City, as "The Big Apple," and soon, even though Emmerich's song was long forgotten, its title became the great city's nickname.

Why is Chicago called the "Windy City"?

Most people believe that Chicago got its nickname from its prevailing winds, but that isn't the case. In 1893, Chicago hosted the World's Columbian Exposition, celebrating the four hundredth anniversary of America's discovery. The city's aggressive promotional campaign for the event offended the people of New York, whose press nicknamed it the Windy City to mock its bragging ways. The moniker stuck, but, fortunately for Chicago, its original meaning has been forgotten by most.

Why are the Southern United States called "Dixieland"?

The nickname "Dixieland" didn't come from the Mason-Dixon Line, the boundary between the free and the slave states. Rather it's from the word *dixie*, which was what southerners called a French ten-dollar bank note of New Orleans that was already in use in 1859 when Daniel Emmet, a northern black man, wrote and introduced his song "Dixie," which spread the South's nickname and somehow became a battle song for the Confederacy.

How did an English police force become known as "Scotland Yard"?

In the tenth century, in an effort to stop hostilities between their two countries, the English gave a Scottish king land in London with the provision that he build a castle on it and live there for a few months every year. Seven centuries later, with the two nations united under one king, the land returned to English ownership. In 1829, the London police took up residence on the land, which by then was known as Scotland Yard.

Why is the American presidential home called the "White House"?

From 1800, when John Adams became the first president to inhabit it, until 1814, when the British burned it because the Americans had torched Toronto, the presidential building was a grey Virginia freestone. It was painted white to cover up the fire damage done by the British. It wasn't officially called the White House until Teddy Roosevelt began printing its image on the executive mansion stationery in 1901.

How did the centre of world commerce, Wall Street, get its name?

In September of 1653, the settlers in what is now New York City felt threatened by the local Natives and by the possibility of an invasion by Oliver Cromwell's army. For protection, they built a large protective wall that stretched a half-mile across Manhattan Island. That wall was situated on the exact spot that we now know as the financial centre of the world: Wall Street.

How did the centre of the song publishing industry become known as "Tin Pan Alley"?

Tin Pan Alley is an actual place in New York City. It's the nickname for the side streets off Times Square, where for generations music publishers have auditioned new songs. The name came from the late 1800s, when the awful sound of cheap tinny pianos coming through the open office windows of hundreds of publishers was likened to the beating of tin pans.

Why are the people of Oklahoma called "Sooners"?

In the 1800s, when the American West was first opened, the early pioneers were offered free land east of the Rockies, but to ensure fairness, they could only stake out forty acres after a race to the region on a specific date and time. Those heading for Oklahoma who jumped the gun and settled on the best land before the official start of the race were cheating and were called "Sooners" because they arrived "sooner" than those who obeyed the law.

Why do we say, "When in Rome, do as the Romans do"?

If you wish to gain esteem and avoid grief, then it's wise to respect the customs of the majority within any culture you may find yourself.

When St. Ambrose was sent on a mission to Rome by St. Augustine, he was concerned about which holy day to observe since the Romans fasted on a different day than was his custom. St. Augustine's wise advice is still with us: "When in Rome, do as the Romans do."

How did feminists come up with the expression "male chauvinist pig"?

The word *chauvinism* originally meant excessive patriotism and came from the name of Nicolas Chauvin, a French general who was known

for his extreme devotion to Napoleon Bonaparte. "Male chauvinism" became a description of a man preoccupied with masculine pursuits during the 1950s, and the word *pig*, borrowed from a slur on policemen, was added by the women's movement in the 1970s.

Why do we call prostitutes "hookers"?

It's a myth that the camp followers of Union General Joseph Hooker gave us the popular euphemism for a prostitute. It's true they were called "Hooker's division," or "Hooker's reserves," but the word predates the American Civil War as, of course, does the profession. It first appeared in 1845 as a reference to an area of New York known as "the Hook," where ladies of the night could be found in abundance.

What exactly is a "family circle"?

When the early Normans brought fire indoors they built semicircular open fireplaces. To keep warm at night or when the air was cool, the family would sit in a semicircle opposite the one formed by the hearth, creating a complete circle where they would spend time telling stories or singing songs within what they called the "family circle." When neighbours were included, it became "a circle of friends."

Why is a self-employed professional called a "freelancer"?

The word *freelance* came out of the period between the fourteenth and sixteenth centuries, when mercenary knights with no particular allegiance would take their lances into battle for the prince or state that paid them the most money. They were referred to as freelancers by authors in the nineteenth century and operated much like the gunfighters in the American West. Now, a freelancer is anyone who works independently.

Why do we call an enthusiastic amateur a "buff"?

A *buff* is someone with a keen interest in a subject that is not related to his or her profession. The term was coined by New York firemen, who were often hindered by crowds who gathered at fires either to help or stand around and criticize. At the time, around 1900, most winter coats worn by the spectators were made of buffalo hide, and from those the firemen came up with the derogatory term "buffs" to describe those pesky amateur critics.

Why do we call wealthy members of society "the upper crust"?

In the days of feudalism, when noblemen gathered for a meal in the castle, those of higher rank sat at the head of a T-shaped table, and the rest sat in order of diminishing importance away from them. For such occasions a yard-long loaf of bread was baked, and the honour of making the first cut belonged to the highest-ranking person at the head table, who would then pass the bread down in order of rank, but always keeping for himself the "upper crust."

Why is a lazy, irresponsible person called "shiftless"?

The word *shift* means to change or rearrange, which is why we call those who work during differing blocks of time "shift workers." This use of the word *shift* also applies to an individual's ability to change or adapt. Therefore, if you're "shiftless" you lack the initiative or resources to change with the circumstances. On the other hand, someone who is "shifty" is too adept at change and isn't to be trusted.

Why do we say that someone with a hidden agenda has "an axe to grind"?

As a boy, Benjamin Franklin was sharpening tools in his father's yard when a stranger carrying an axe came by and praised the boy on how good he was with the grindstone. He then asked Franklin if he would show him how it would work on his own axe. Once his axe was sharpened, the stranger simply laughed and walked away, giving young Franklin a valuable lesson about people with "an axe to grind."

Why is a newcomer called a "rookie"?

A *rookie* is anyone new to an organization requiring teamwork and whose lack of experience may cause errors. The word originated in the American military during the Civil War when massive numbers of young and untrained soldiers were rushed into battle, causing major problems with discipline. The veterans called these incompetents "reckies," an abbreviation of *recruits*, which through time became "rookies."

Why are strangers who plead for help called "beggars"?

The name of a twelfth-century monk, Lambert de Begue, whose followers wandered the French countryside depending on handouts, gave us the verb *to beg*. When in 555 AD the Roman general Belisarius was stripped of his rank and wealth, he became one of history's most notable beggars, and his frequent cry, "Don't kick a man when he's down," gave us a maxim for all who are on very hard times.

Why is someone who challenges what appears to be an obvious truth called a "devil's advocate"?

During the Roman Catholic proceedings leading to the assignment of sainthood, a specific individual is given the job of investigating the candidate and the validity of any associated miracles. He then argues vehemently against the canonization by denigrating the potential saint on behalf of the devil. His official Vatican title is the "Devil's Advocate."

Why do we call someone who does things differently a "maverick"?

In the nineteenth century, Samuel A. Maverick was a stubborn Texas rancher who, because he said it was cruel, refused to brand his cattle even though it was the only way to identify who owned free-range livestock. Instead he would round up all the unbranded cattle he could find, even those not from his own herd. At first any stray unbranded cow was called a "maverick," but the word has grown to mean anyone who doesn't play by the rules.

Why is a college student in her second year referred to as a "sophomore"?

After her first, or "freshman," year, a college student is called a "sophomore," and has been since the description emerged at Cambridge in 1688. The word is constructed from the Greek *sophos*, meaning wise, and *moros*, meaning foolish. So a second-year student is somewhere between ignorance and wisdom. Similarly, when we say something is "sophomoric," we mean it is pretentious or foolish.

Why is a private detective called a "private eye"?

In 1850, the Pinkerton Detective Agency opened in Chicago with the slogan "We never sleep," and its symbol was a large wide-open eye. Pinkerton was very effective and criminals began calling the feared operation "the eye." Raymond Chandler and other fiction writers of the 1930s and 1940s simply embellished the underworld expression by introducing "private eye" as a description for any private investigator.

Why are women temporarily separated from their husbands called "grass widows"?

The expression *grass widow* originated hundreds of years ago in Europe where summers were unbearably hot. Because grass was scarce in the lowlands, husbands would send their wives and children, along with their resting workhorses, up into the cooler grassy uplands while they stayed in the heat to till the land. It was said that both the wives and horses had been "sent to grass," which gave us the expression *grass widows*.

Why does a man refer to his wife as his "better half"?

Most men call their wives their "better half" because they believe it, but the expression comes from an ancient Middle Eastern legend. When a Bedouin man had been sentenced to death, his wife pleaded with the tribal leader that because they were married, she and her husband had become one, and that to punish one-half of the union would also punish the half who was innocent. The court agreed and the man's life was saved by his "better half."

Why are women referred to as the "distaff" side of a family?

In medieval times the marriage bargain held men responsible for the physical labour outside of the home, while the women provided nourishment and comfort inside. A *distaff* was a rod used to hold wool during weaving and became a symbol of honour and respect to the value of a woman's work toward the family's well-being. The equal to the female "distaff-side" is the male "spear-side."

Why do Mexicans call Americans "gringos"?

Some say that during the Mexican-American war at the end of the nineteenth century, locals heard the invaders singing "Green Grow the Lilacs" and simply picked up "gringo" from "green grow." Others say that because the American uniforms were green, the expression came from a rallying cry: "Green, go!" But, in fact, *gringo* is a Spanish word on its own and is a slang insult for anyone who is fair-skinned and looks foreign.

Why is someone with a lot of nerve referred to as being "full of moxie"?

Today Moxie is a New England soft drink, but it began as a tonic invented by Dr. Augustine Thompson in 1884 as "Moxie Nerve Food." Although the 1906 *Pure Food and Drug Act* put an end to its medicinal claims, there are still those who say Moxie gives them energy, and so to be "full of moxie" means to be full of false nerve.

What does the title *esquire* mean?

The British title *esquire*, like the magazine, has very masculine roots. An esquire was a young man who was a manservant to an armoured knight and whose job included holding his master's shield. With the passing of the knights, *esquire* was applied to any young man of noble birth who hadn't yet earned a proper title. Eventually the word became a term of respect for any promising young man.

Why do we call someone who continually takes the fall for someone else a "whipping boy"?

In the mid-seventeenth century, young princes and aristocrats were sent off to school with a young servant who would attend classes and receive an education while also attending to his master's needs. If the master found himself in trouble, the servant would take the punishment for him, even if it were a whipping. He was his master's "whipping boy."

Why is the word *late* used to describe the recently deceased?

To prefix a person's name with "the late" certainly signifies that he or she is dead, although you would be correct in using it only with the name of someone who had died within the past twenty years. Its use began with medieval rulers, whose first name often had been passed down through generations of males. To avoid confusion with the living monarch, i.e., James II, his deceased father would be referred to as "the late King James."

How did the word *gay* come to mean homosexual?

The word *gay* is from the Old French *gai*, meaning "merry." It came to mean reckless self-indulgence in the seventeenth century, and it wasn't until the 1930s that its homosexual connotation came out of the prison system, where the expression "gay-cat" meant a younger, inexperienced man who, in order to survive, traded his virtue for the protection and experience of an older convict.

When a man gifted with charm seizes an opportunity, why do we say, "He's in like Flynn"?

The Australian actor Errol Flynn had an amazing prowess with the ladies, and of course the tabloids built this into a legend. During the Second World War, servicemen coined the phrase "in like Flynn" either to brag about their own conquests or to describe someone they envied. Flynn said he hated the expression, but his own boast that he had spent between twelve and fourteen thousand intimate nights ensured its survival.

Why do we say that someone who inherited wealth was "born with a silver spoon in his mouth"?

If someone is "born with a silver spoon in his mouth," it means that he was born into wealth rather than having had to earn it. The expression comes from an old custom of godparents giving the gift of a spoon to a child at its christening to signify their responsibility for its nourishment and well-being. If they were wealthy, the spoon was usually silver, and if not, it would be pewter or tin.

Why do we call a cowardly person "yellow"?

Yellow, meaning cowardly, is actually an abbreviation of *yellow dog*, an American insult that first appeared in the nineteenth century to describe a cowardly or worthless person. In the early twentieth century, when employers were fighting trade unions, they insisted that new employees sign a pledge never to join a union. This pledge was called a "yellow dog" contract by union members with the implication that anyone signing it was "yellow."

POP CULTURE

How did Clark Kent get his name?

When conceived in 1934, Superman was endowed with the strength of ten men, but he couldn't fly. After being turned down by fifteen syndicators, the Man of Steel took to the air and acquired the needed strength to become a super legend. Some say Superman's success is within the storyline of his secret identity, whose name was derived from two popular actors of the time: "Clark" Gable and "Kent" Taylor.

Who was Mortimer Mouse and whatever happened to him?

Mortimer was Walt Disney's original name for a cartoon mouse in the historic 1928 cartoon "Plane Crazy." When Walt came home and told his wife about the little mouse, she didn't like the name "Mortimer" and suggested that "Mickey" was more pleasant-sounding. Walt thought about it for a while and then grudgingly gave in, and that's how Mickey, and not Mortimer, went on to become the foundation of an entertainment empire.

How did the cartoon character Bugs Bunny get his name?

In 1940, Warner Bros. asked its illustrators for sketches of a "tall, lanky, mean rabbit" for a cartoon titled "Hare-um Scare-um." Someone in the office labelled the submission from cartoonist "Bugs" Hardaway as "Bugs' Bunny" and sent it on. Although his drawings weren't used, the words that labelled them were given to the rabbit star of the 1940 cartoon "A Wild Hare," which introduced "Bugs Bunny."

How did the Wizard Of Oz get that name?

The classic tale of Dorothy in the land of Oz came from the imagination of L. Frank Baum, who made up the story for his son and a group of children one evening in 1899. When a little girl asked him the name of this magical land with the Scarecrow, Tinman, and Cowardly Lion, he looked around the room for inspiration. He happened to be sitting next to a filing cabinet with the drawers labelled "A-G," "H-N," and finally "O-Z," which gave him a quick answer: "Oz."

How did the name *Wendy* originate?

The name *Wendy* was invented by J.M. Barrie for a character in his 1904 play *Peter Pan*. The poet W.E. Henley, a close friend of Barrie's, had a four-year-old daughter, Margaret, and because her father always referred to Barrie as "friend," she would try to imitate him by saying "fwend" or "fwendy-wendy." Sadly, Margaret died at the age of six, but her expression lives on in *Peter Pan* and all the Wendys that have followed.

Have you ever wondered how Cinderella could have walked in a glass slipper?

The story of Cinderella was passed along orally for centuries before it was written down by Charles Perrault in 1697. While doing so he mistook the word *vair*, meaning ermine, for the word *verre*, meaning glass. By the time he realized his mistake, the story had become too popular to change, and so instead of an ermine slipper, Cinderella wore glass.

Why is a beautiful blonde called a "blonde bombshell"?

The expression "blonde bombshell," often used to describe a dynamic and sexy woman with blonde hair, came from a 1933 movie starring Jean Harlow. Hollywood first titled the film *Bombshell*, but because it sounded like a war film, the British changed the title to *Blonde Bombshell*. It originally referred only to the platinum-haired Miss Harlow, but has come to mean any gorgeous woman of the blonde persuasion.

How many movies are made annually in Hollywood?

There hasn't been a movie made in Hollywood since 1911, when, fed up with ramshackle sets and the chaotic influence of hordes of actors and crews, the town tossed out the Nestor Film Company and wrote an ordinance forbidding the building of any future studios. Even so, the magic of the name was already established, and so the industry we call Hollywood grew up around that little town in such places as Burbank, Santa Monica, and Culver City — but not in Hollywood.

Why do we call Academy Awards "Oscars"?

Since 1928, the Academy Awards have been issued by the American Academy of Motion Picture Arts and Sciences for excellence in filmmaking. The statuettes were nicknamed "Oscar" in 1931 by Margaret Herrick, a secretary at the academy who, upon seeing one for the first time, exclaimed, "Why it looks just like my uncle Oscar." Her uncle was Oscar Pierce, a wheat farmer.

Who was Mona Lisa in da Vinci's famous masterpiece?

Although it's known as the *Mona Lisa*, Leonardo da Vinci's famous painting was originally titled *La Giaconda*. Painted on wood, it's a portrait of Lisa Gherardini, the wife of a Florentine merchant. X-rays reveal that Leonardo sketched three different poses before settling on the final design. The painting of Lisa has no eyebrows because it was the fashion of the time for women to shave them off.

What is the most popular rock and roll song in history?

Because the lyrics in the Kingsmen's 1963 recording of the song "Louie, Louie" were unintelligible, people thought they were dirty, and although they weren't, a U.S. congressional investigation assured the song's enduring success. Since being sold by its author, Richard Berry, for $750 in 1957, "Louie, Louie" has been recorded by nearly one thousand different performers and sold an estimated quarter-billion copies.

Who owns the song "Happy Birthday"?

"Happy Birthday" began as "Good Morning Dear Children" and was written by educators Mildred and Patty Hill in 1893. In 1924, a publisher changed the opening line to "Happy Birthday to You" and it became a ritual to sing the song to anyone celebrating his or her birthday. In 1934, after hearing the song in a Broadway musical, a third Hill sister, Jessica, sued the show and won. The Hill family was thereafter entitled to royalties whenever the melody was performed commercially.

What's unusual about the music to the American national anthem?

In 1814, after a night in a pub, Francis Scott Key was taken prisoner during the war between Canada and the United States. When he saw the American flag still flying over Fort McHenry he was inspired to write his famous lyrics with one particular barroom song, "To Anacreon In Heaven," still in his mind. And so "The Star Spangled Banner" was written to the tune of a traditional old English drinking song.

Who was Matilda in the song "Waltzing Matilda"?

In the Australian song "Waltzing Matilda," a *billabong* is a pool of stagnant water. A *swagman* was someone who carried around everything he owned in a knapsack. *Waltzing* meant hiking, and *Matilda* wasn't a woman but rather an Australian word for a knapsack. So Waltzing Matilda means: walking with my knapsack.

How did the poem "Mary Had a Little Lamb" become so famous?

"Mary Had a Little Lamb" was written in 1830 by Sarah Hale, the editor of *Godey's Ladies Magazine*. She was inspired after watching young Mary Tyler's pet lamb follow the girl to school, which, of course, was against the rules. The poem became immortal more than fifty years later when Thomas Edison used it as the first words ever spoken and then recorded on his new invention, the phonograph.

Who was Little Jack Horner in the nursery rhyme?

At a time when Henry VIII was confiscating church property, one monk appeased the king with the gift of a special Christmas pie. Inside the crust were deeds to twelve manor houses secretly offered in exchange for his monastery. The steward who carried the pie to London was Jack Horner, who along the way extracted a plum deed for himself. It was for Mells Manor, where Horner's descendants still live to this day.

Where did the bearded figure Uncle Sam come from?

Sam Wilson was a meat packer who supplied preserved beef to the U.S. Army in the nineteenth century. The barrels of meat were stamped "U.S." to indicate they were property of the United States, but the soldiers joked that the initials were actually those of the supplier, "Uncle Sam" Wilson. The bearded figure of "Uncle Sam" was drawn and introduced by Thomas Nast, the same cartoonist who created the Republicans' elephant and the Democrats' donkey.

How did the Mercedes automobile get its name?

In 1900, the Daimler Corporation was commissioned to design and build a special racing car to add to the fleet of a wealthy Austrian named Emil Jellinek. Mr. Jellinek gave the special car the nickname "Mercedes," which was his daughter's name. Jellinek was so impressed with the car that he bought into Daimler, and when the company merged with Benz in 1926, company officials decided to keep the name and market a commercial car as the Mercedes Benz.

Why were dancers in the thirties and forties called "jitterbugs"?

Band leader Cab Calloway coined the word *jitterbug* as a description of both the music and the dancers during the big band era. It came from a time when drinking alcohol was prohibited by law, giving rise to the popularity of illegal booze. Because of its hangover effect, moonshine had long been called "jitter sauce," and Calloway, while watching the intoxicated dancers, labelled them "jitterbugs."

How did the soft drink Dr. Pepper get its name?

In Virginia in the 1880s, Wade Morrison, a pharmacist's assistant, wanted to marry his boss's daughter. But her father considered Morrison too old for her and asked him to move on. After Morrison had settled down and opened his own drugstore in Waco, Texas, one of his employees came up with a new soft drink idea, which Morrison developed and named after the man who gave him his start in the drug business: his old girlfriend's father, Dr. Kenneth Pepper.

How did the drink Gatorade get its name?

In 1963, Dr. Robert Cade was studying the effects of heat exhaustion on football players at the University of Florida. After analyzing the body liquids lost during sweating, Cade quickly came up with a formula for a drink to replace them. Within two years, Gatorade was a $50-million business. The doctor named his new health drink after the football team he used in his study, the Florida Gators.

Why do we call a bad actor a "ham" and silly comedy "slapstick"?

In the late nineteenth century, second-rate actors couldn't afford cold cream to remove their stage makeup, so they used ham fat and were called hamfatters until early in the twentieth century when these bad actors were simply called "hams." Physical comedy became known as "slapstick" because of its regular use of crude sound effects: two sticks were slapped together off-stage to accentuate a comic's onstage pratfall (*prat* being an Old English term for buttocks).

Why are vain people said to be "looking for the limelight"?

In the early days of theatre, the players were lit by gas lamps hidden across the front of the stage. Early in the twentieth century, it was discovered that if a stick of lime was added to the gas, the light became more intense, and so they began to use the "limelight" to illuminate the spot on stage where the most important part of the play took place. Later called the "spotlight," the "limelight" was where all actors fought to be.

How did teenagers become a separate culture?

The word *teenager* first appeared in 1941, but the emancipation of that age group began forty years earlier when new laws freed children from hard labour and kept them in school. Until then, there was only childhood and adulthood. At the age of thirteen, a girl became a woman and could marry or enter the workforce and a boy became a man. Today, teenagers are treated as children with suppressed adult urges.

Why is a formal suit for men called a "tuxedo"?

In the nineteenth century, the accepted formal dress for men was a suit with long swallowtails. But one evening in 1886, young Griswald

Lorillard, the heir to a tobacco fortune, shocked his country club by arriving in a dinner jacket without tails. This fashion statement caught on, and the suit took on the name the place Lorillard introduced it: Tuxedo Park, New Jersey.

Where did the coffee habit come from?

Muslims were the first to develop coffee. As early as 1524 they were using it as a replacement for the wine they were forbidden to drink. According to legend, an astute Arab herder noticed that his goats became skittish after chewing on the berries of a certain bush, so he sampled a few himself and found them to be invigorating. The region of Abyssinia where this took place is named Kaffa, which gave us the name for the drink we call coffee.

Why do we define the rat race as "keeping up with the Joneses"?

Keeping up with the Joneses has come to mean trying to keep up with your neighbours, in terms of material possessions, at any cost. The expression comes from the title of a comic strip that ran in newspapers between 1913 and 1931 and chronicled the experiences of a newly married man in Cedarhurst, New York. Originally titled "Keeping Up With the Smiths," the cartoon was changed to the "Keeping Up With the Joneses" because it sounded better.

CUSTOMS

Why do we say "Hello" when we answer the telephone?

The first word used to answer the phone was the nautical greeting "ahoy" because the first regular phone system was in the maritime state of Connecticut. Alexander Graham Bell, the inventor, answered with the Gaelic "hoy," but it was Thomas Edison's greeting of "hello," an exclamation of surprise dating back to the Middle Ages, that caught on, and so we answer today with, "Hello?"

Why do we say "goodbye" or "so long" when leaving someone?

The word *goodbye* is a derivative of the early English greeting "God be with you," or as it was said then, "God be with ye." Over the years its abbreviated written form and pronunciation became "goodbye." As for "so long," it came to Britain with soldiers who had spent time in Arabic-speaking countries, where the perfect expression of goodwill is "salaam." The unfamiliar word to the English men sounded like, and then became, "so long."

When did men start shaving every morning?

In many cultures shaving is forbidden. The reason we in the West lather up every morning can be traced directly back to Alexander the Great. Before he seized power, all European men grew beards. But because young Alexander wasn't able to muster much facial hair, he scraped off his peach fuzz every day with a dagger. Not wanting to offend the great warrior, those close to him did likewise, and soon shaving became the custom.

Why do men wear neckties?

Roman soldiers wore a strip of cloth around their necks to keep them warm in winter and to absorb sweat in the summer. Other armies followed suit, and during the French Revolution the Royalists and the Rebels used ties to display the colours of their allegiance. They borrowed the design and the name, *cravat*, from the Croatian Army. Later, ties became a French fashion statement, offering a splash of colour to an otherwise drab wardrobe.

Why are men's buttons on the right and women's on the left?

Decorative buttons first appeared around 2000 BC, but they weren't commonly used as fasteners until the sixteenth century. Because most men are right-handed and generally dressed themselves, they found it easier to fasten their buttons from right to left. However, wealthy women were dressed by servants, who found it easier to fasten their mistresses' clothes if the buttons were on her left. It became convention and has never changed.

Why do baby boys wear blue and girls wear pink?

The custom of dressing baby boys in blue clothes began around 1400. Blue was the colour of the sky and therefore Heaven, so it was believed that the colour warded off evil spirits. Male children were considered a greater blessing than females, so it was assumed that demons had no interest in girls. It was another hundred years before girls were given red as a colour, which was later softened to pink.

Why is a handshake considered to be a gesture of friendship?

The Egyptian hieroglyph for "to give" is an extended hand. That symbol was the inspiration for Michelangelo's famous fresco "The Creation of Adam," which is found on the ceiling of the Sistine Chapel. Babylonian kings confirmed their authority by annually grasping the hand of a statue of their chief god, Marduk. The handshake as we know it today evolved from a custom of Roman soldiers, who carried daggers in their right wristbands. They would extend and then grasp each other's weapon hand as a non-threatening sign of goodwill.

Where did the two-fingered peace sign come from?

The gesture of two fingers spread and raised in peace, popularized in the 1960s, is a physical interpretation of the peace symbol, an inverted or upside-down Y within a circle, which was designed in 1958 by members of the anti-nuclear Direct Action Committee. The inverted Y is a combination of the maritime semaphore signals for N and D, which stood for "nuclear disarmament."

Where did the rude Anglo-Saxon one-fingered salute come from?

When the outnumbered English faced the French at the Battle of Agincourt, they were armed with a relatively new weapon, the longbow. The French were so amused that they vowed to cut off the middle finger of each British archer. When the longbows won the day, the English jeered the retreating French by raising that middle finger in a gesture that still means, among other things, "in your face."

Why do Christians place their hands together in prayer?

The original gesture of Christian prayer was spreading the arms and hands heavenward. There is no mention anywhere in the Bible of joining hands in prayer, and that custom didn't surface in the church until the ninth century. In Roman times, a man would place his hands together as an offer of submission that meant, "I surrender, here are my hands ready to be bound or shackled." Christianity accepted the gesture as a symbol of offering total obedience, or submission, to God.

Why was grace originally a prayer said after a meal?

Today, we say grace before a meal in thanksgiving for an abundance of food, but in ancient times, food spoiled quickly, often causing illness or even death. Nomadic tribes experimenting with unfamiliar plants were very often poisoned. Before a meal, these people made a plea to the gods to deliver them from poisoning, but it wasn't until after the meal, if everyone was still standing, that they offered a prayer of thanksgiving, or "grace."

Why at the end of a profound statement or prayer do Christians, Moslems, and Jews all say "amen?"

The word *amen* appears 13 times in the Hebrew Bible and 119 times in the New Testament as well as in the earliest Moslem writings. The word originated in Egypt around 2500 BC as *Amun*, and meant the "Hidden One," the name of their highest deity. Hebrew scholars adopted the word as meaning "so it is" and passed it on to the Christians and Moslems.

Why is June the most popular month for weddings?

The ancient Greeks and Romans both suggested marriage during a full moon because of its positive influence on fertility. The Romans favoured June, a month they named after Juno, the goddess of marriage, because if the bride conceived right away, she wouldn't be too pregnant to help with the harvest. She also would probably have recovered from giving birth in time to help in the fields with the next year's harvest.

Why are wedding banns announced before a marriage?

The custom of proclaiming wedding banns began in 800 AD when Roman Emperor Charlemagne became alarmed by the high rate of interbreeding throughout his empire. He ordered that all marriages be publicly announced at least seven days prior to the ceremony and that anyone knowing that the bride and groom were related must come forward. The practice proved so successful that it was widely endorsed by all faiths.

Why does a groom carry his bride over the threshold?

The custom of carrying a bride over the threshold comes from the kidnapping practices of the Germanic Goths around 200 AD. Generally, these men only married women from within their own communities, but when the supply ran short, they would raid neighbouring villages and seize young girls to carry home as their wives. From this practice of abduction sprang the now symbolic act of carrying the bride over the threshold.

Why do brides wear "something old, something new, something borrowed, and something blue" to their weddings?

According to wedding tradition, the bride wears something "old" to remind the couple of the happiness of the courting period. She wears something "new" to represent the hopeful success of the couple's new life together; something "borrowed" to symbolize the support of friends; and something "blue" because it's the colour of fidelity. If a bride wears a single girlfriend's garter, it will improve that girl's prospects of marriage.

Why do bridegrooms have a best man?

In ancient times, most marriages were arranged, and so the groom wasn't always the bride's first choice. The man she favoured would often swear to carry her off before or during the wedding. To avoid this, the groom stood on the bride's right to keep his sword arm free and would enlist a warrior companion to fight off the rival if he showed up. This companion was, in fact, the "best man."

Why is a wedding reception called a "bridal" party?

The expressions *bridal feast*, *bridal bed*, and *bridal cake*, among other bridal references, all date back to around 1200, when a wedding was a rather boisterous and bawdy affair. The word *bridal* comes from "bride-ale," which was the special beer brewed for the wedding and then sold to the guests to raise money for the newlyweds. Because of the bride-ale, weddings were quite rowdy until around the seventeenth century, when the church managed to get a grip on the whole thing.

Why do we drink a toast on special occasions?

By the sixth century BC, Greeks had discovered that poisoning wine was an excellent way to get rid of their enemies, and so to reassure guests at a social function, it became necessary for the host to take the first drink. The Romans added a piece of burnt bread, or "tostus," to the custom because it absorbed acid, making the wine more pleasant to drink. Flattering words were spoken during the toasting ceremony to reassure the guests of their safety.

Why does everyone touch wine glasses before drinking at a dinner party?

The custom of touching wine glasses comes from a medieval host's precaution against being poisoned by a guest, or vice versa. The original ritual was that while touching glasses, a little wine was exchanged, poured from one goblet into the other, around the table. Then everyone took their first drink at the same time. By mixing drinks this way, the host and everyone else could be assured that no assassin was in their midst.

Why do we roll out a red carpet for special guests?

The red carpet treatment dates back to the 1930s, when a carpet of that colour led passengers to a luxurious train, the *Twentieth Century Limited*, which ran between New York and Chicago. The *Twentieth Century* was the most famous in America and was totally first class with accommodation and dining car menus that were considered the height of luxury. Walking the red carpet to the train meant you were about to be treated like royalty.

Why do we put candles on a birthday cake?

The Greeks borrowed celebrating birthdays from the Egyptian

pharaohs and the cake idea from the Persians. Then early Christians did away with birthday parties for a while until the custom re-emerged with candles in Germany in the twelfth century. Awakened with the arrival of a birthday cake topped with lighted candles, which were changed and kept lit until after the family meal, the honoured child would make a wish that, it was said, would come true only if the candles were blown out in a single breath.

How did wakes become part of the funeral tradition?

The Irish are the most famous for their wakes, holding elaborate and festive celebrations with testimonials and toasts to the recently deceased. The custom began long before the advances of scientific undertaking and was a way of passing enough time to ensure that the subject wasn't about to be buried alive. The ritual was held to see if the subject would wake up, which sometimes happened, and so it was called a "wake."

Why are flags flown at half-staff?

In the sixteenth century, ships would lower their flag halfway as a sign of submission during battle, and it was said they were flying at "half-mast." On reaching port, the flag remained half-lowered in honour of those who had sacrificed their lives. In the seventeenth century the ritual moved to land, where it was said the flags were at "half-staff," as a sign of respect for any individual who had died serving his country beyond the call of duty.

Why do funeral processions move so slowly?

The Romans introduced the lighting of candles and torches at funeral services to ward off evil spirits and guide the deceased to paradise. The word *funeral* itself is derived from the Latin word for torch. By the fifteenth century, people were placing huge candelabras on the coffin even as it was carried to the burial ground. The funeral procession moved at a very slow pace so that the candles wouldn't blow out.

Why do the British drive on the left side of the road while Americans use the right?

The British custom of driving on the left was passed down from the Romans. The chariot driver stayed to the left in order to meet an approaching enemy with his right sword hand. Americans switched to driving on the right because on covered wagons, the brakes were built on the left, forcing the driver to sit on that same side and, consequently, to drive on the right so they could have a clear view of the road.

Why do we use Xs as kisses at the bottom of a letter?

During medieval times, most people could neither read nor write, and even those who could sign their names were required to follow it with an X, symbolizing the cross of St. Andrew, or the contract would be invalid. Those who couldn't write their names still had to end the contract with the X to make it legal. To prove their intention, all were required to kiss the cross, which through time is how the X became associated with a lover's kiss.

How did we start the ritual of kissing a wound to make it better?

Everyone with children has kissed a small bruise or cut to make it better. This comes from one of our earliest medical procedures for the treatment of snakebite. Noticing that a victim could be saved if the venom was sucked out through the point of entry, early doctors soon began treating all infectious abrasions by putting their lips to the wound and sucking out the poison. Medicine moved on, but the belief that a kiss can make it all better still lingers.

How did flipping a coin become a decision-maker?

The Lydians minted the first coins in 10 BC but it wasn't until nine hundred years later that the coin toss became a decision-maker. Julius Caesar's head appeared on one side of every Roman coin of his time, and such was the reverence for the emperor that in his absence often serious litigation was decided by the flip of a coin. If Caesar's head landed upright, it meant that through the guidance of the gods, he agreed in absentia with the decision in question.

SPORTS & LEISURE

Why is the Cleveland baseball team called the Indians?

Controversy generally surrounds the choice of Native American names for sports teams, but not in Cleveland. That city's baseball team is named in honour of one of their star players from the 1890s. He was Alex Sophalexis, a Penobscot Indian so respected that in 1914, one year after his death, Cleveland took the name "Indians" to commemorate Alex and what he had meant to their team.

Why is the L.A. baseball team called the Dodgers?

Before moving to Los Angeles, the Dodgers were based in Brooklyn, New York. The team had originated in the nineteenth century when, because of the dangers of horse-drawn trolleys and carriages, the pedestrians of Brooklyn called themselves "trolley dodgers." Because most of their working-class fans had to dodge traffic on their walk to the games, the Brooklyn baseball team named themselves the "Dodgers" in their honour. When the team moved to L.A. in the 1950s, they took the name with them.

Why does the letter *K* signify a strikeout on a baseball scoresheet?

Early in baseball history, a man named Henry Chadwick designed the system we still use for keeping score. Because his system already had an overabundance of *S*s scattered throughout his scoresheet — safe, slide, shortstop, sacrifice, second base, etc. — he decided to use the last letter of *struck*, as in, "he struck out," rather than the first. And that's why *K* signifies a strikeout in baseball.

Why do we call someone who is left-handed a "southpaw"?

When the first baseball diamonds were laid out there were no night games. To keep the afternoon or setting sun out of the batters' eyes, home plate was positioned so that the hitter was facing east, which meant the pitcher was facing west. Most pitchers threw with their right arm, but the rare and dreaded left-hander's pitching arm was on the more unfamiliar south side, and he was referred to, with respect, as a southpaw.

Why is an erratic person called a "screwball"?

In baseball, when a pitcher throws a curveball, it breaks to a right-handers left and a left-handers right. Early in the twentieth century, the great Christy Mathewson came up with a pitch that broke in the opposite direction and completely baffled opposing batters, who called it a "screwball." It became a word used to describe anything eccentric or totally surprising — including some humans.

Why in sports does the home team wear white while the visitors wear darker colours?

Early television was in black and white and the definitions weren't nearly as precise as they are today. When the Canadian Broadcasting Corporation was testing for live hockey broadcasts in 1952, they found that if both teams wore their traditional colours, it was impossible to tell them apart. They solved the problem by having the home team wear white, while the visitors stayed in their darker uniforms.

Why is a football field called a "gridiron"?

The word *football* first described a game involving two teams and an inflated animal bladder in 1486. The game evolved several times before North Americans introduced new rules, such as three chances to advance the ball five yards, that led to white lines being painted on the field. From the stands, these lines gave the field the appearance of broiled meat from the metal grating of a griddle or "gridiron," and so that's what they called it.

Why isn't it over 'til the fat lady sings?

In the 1970s, Washington sports columnist Dan Cook wrote, "The opera isn't over 'til the fat lady sings." Later, basketball coach Dick Motta, referring to the Bulls' slim playoff chances, misquoted Cook when he said, "It isn't over 'til the fat lady sings," and it stuck. The inspiration might have been the old American proverb, "Church ain't out 'til the fat lady sings," but regardless, it's now accepted in sports as meaning: where there's life, there's hope.

Where did we get the expression *second string?*

In sports jargon, the *second string* is the second-best group of players on a given team. The term has also found its way into business, where it is used in much the same way. In fact, it comes from medieval archers, who always carried an extra string in case the one on their bow broke. Therefore the second string had to be as good as the first, as did the third and fourth strings.

Why do we say a person isn't "up to scratch?"

During the early days of bare-knuckle boxing, a line was scratched across the centre of the ring, dividing it into two halves. This is where the fighters met to start the contest, or where they "toed the line" to begin each round. If, as the fight progressed, one of the boxers was unable to toe the line without help from his seconds, it was said he had failed to come "up to scratch."

Why is a boxing ring square?

In the days of bare-knuckle boxing, before modern rules, a circle was drawn in the dirt and prize fighters were ringed by the fans. When one of the men was knocked out of that circle, he was simply pushed back into the ring by the crowd. In 1867, Marcus of Queensbury introduced a number of rules to boxing, including three-minute rounds and a roped-off square, which fans continued to call the "boxing ring."

Why do we call the genuine article "the real McCoy"?

In the 1890s, a great boxer known as Kid McCoy couldn't get the champion to fight him, and so to seem beatable, he began to throw the odd bout, and fans never knew if they'd see the "real McCoy." The plan worked, and he became the welterweight champion of the world.

Once, while in a bar, McCoy was challenged by a drunken patron who didn't believe that he was the great boxer, and McCoy flattened him. When the man came around, he declared that the man who had knocked him out was indeed the "real McCoy."

Why is a fistfight called "duking it out"?

"Duking it out" and "Put up your dukes" are both expressions from the early 1800s when bare-knuckle boxing was considered a lower-class activity. When Frederick Augustus, the then duke of York took up the sport, English high society was shocked. The "Duke" gained so much admiration from the other boxers, however, that they began referring to their fists as their "dukes of York" and eventually as their "dukes."

How did tennis get the terms *seeded* and *love*?

Tennis was popularized by the French nobility, and because a zero looked like an egg that's what they called it. *Egg* in French is *l'oeuf*, which became *love* in English. The seeding or placing of the best players within favourable tournament positions required other players to graciously cede — yield or give up — the spots. In time, the word mutated to the spelling of its homonym, *seed*, and so players were said to be *seeded*.

Why are golf assistants called "caddies"?

In medieval France the first-born sons of nobility were known as the "caput," or head, of the family, while the younger, less valuable boys were called "capdets," or little heads, and were often sent to the military to train as officers. In English, "capdets" became "cadets," which the Scots abbreviated to "cads" or "caddies," meaning any useless street kid who could be hired for the day to carry around a bag of golf clubs.

Why is it so difficult for women to join prestigious British golf clubs?

Exclusive men's country clubs were called golf clubs long before the game was invented. "GOLF" is an acronym derived from the phrase "gentlemen only, ladies forbidden." Men had formed these clubs to enjoy themselves without the politics of dealing with women. When they began chasing a small ball around the grounds they gave the game the same name as their club: golf.

Why are billiards played on a pool table?

During the nineteenth century, off-track gamblers would often play billiards while waiting to hear the results of a horse race. Sometimes, if they agreed on the merits of a particular horse, the gamblers would pool their money in an effort to win a greater amount on one bet or to soften the blow of a loss. The "pooled" money, both bet and won, was counted out on the playing surface of the billiard table, which the gamblers came to call their "pool table."

Why, when someone has won without question, do we say that he did it "hands down"?

To win hands down has nothing to do with placing a winning hand of cards face down. Instead, the expression comes from the earliest days of horseracing. If a horse had proven its superiority and was approaching the finish line well ahead of the pack, the jockey would release the reins, giving the animal free reign to the finish. He therefore would win the race "hands down."

Why is a lottery winning called a "jackpot"?

A *jackpot* is any large amount of money won through gambling. The word comes from a game of draw poker in which only a player dealt a pair of jacks or better can open. Several hands are usually dealt before this happens, and with each deal the players must add to the ante, which can grow to a considerable amount of money — the "jack" pot. When two jacks are finally dealt and a player opens the betting, the winner will take the jackpot.

Where did the expression "according to Hoyle" come from?

An Englishman named Edmond Hoyle wrote a rulebook for the card game whist, the ancestor of bridge, in 1742. Hoyle's rules were used to settle arguments during that one game until Robert Foster published *Foster's Hoyle* in 1897, which included the rules for many other card games. Since then, "according to Hoyle" has meant according to the rules of any game, including those played in business and personal relationships.

Why, when someone losing begins to win, do we say he's "turned the tables"?

The phrase "to turn the tables" is a chess term dating from 1634 that describes a sudden recovery by a losing player. The switch in position of each side's pieces makes it look as though the losing player had physically turned the table on his opponent to take over the winning side of the board.

Incidentally, it's impossible to successively double the number of coins on each square of a chessboard. By the time you've finished you would need 18 quintillion coins, more than all that have ever been minted.

Why is a non-relevant statement during a debate or argument said to be "beside the point"?

The expression "beside the point" is from ancient archery and literally means your shot is wide of the target. Its figurative meaning, that your argument is irrelevant, entered the language about 1352, as did "You've missed the mark." Both suggest that regardless of your intentions, your invalid statement is outside the subject under discussion.

Why is a marathon race exactly 26 miles and 385 yards long?

In 1908, the first modern Olympic marathon was designed to start at Windsor Castle and end in front of the royal box in the London stadium, a distance of exactly 26 miles, 385 yards, and that became the official distance. The race honoured Pheidippedes, who in 490 BC had run 22 miles, 1,470 yards to carry news to Athens that the Greeks had defeated the Persians on the plain of Marathon.

Would ancient Greek athletes have had any chance against our well-trained modern Olympians?

At least two ancient Greek athletes would have done well in the modern games; their Olympic records stood until the twentieth century. Twenty-six hundred years ago, an athlete named Protiselaus threw a cumbersome primitive discus 152 feet from a standing position. No one exceeded that distance until Clarence Houser, an American, threw the discus 155 feet in 1928. In 656 BC, a Greek Olympian named Chionis leapt 23 feet, 1.5 inches, a long jump record that stood until 1900, when an American named Alvis Kraenzlein surpassed it by 4.5 inches.

What does it mean to "rest on your laurels"?

The practice of using laurels to symbolize victory came from the ancient Greeks. After winning on the battlefield, great warriors were crowned with a wreath of laurels, or bay leaves, to signify their supreme status during a victory parade. Because the first Olympics consisted largely of war games, the champions were honoured in the same manner: with a laurel, a crown of leaves. To "rest on your laurels" means to quit while you're ahead.

Why is a trophy a symbol of victory?

After a victory on a battlefield, the ancient Greeks would build a monument dedicated to a chosen god, which they called a "trophy." These trophies were made of limbs stripped from the dead enemy soldiers and then hung on a tree or pillar, a ritual that is kept alive by modern "trophy hunters," who celebrate their victory over an unarmed animal by hanging its head on the wall. Be grateful for the Stanley Cup.

Why is a blue ribbon a symbol of champions?

Blue was the favourite colour of England's King Edward III, who in 1348 created the highest Royal Order of the Knights of the Garter. Its membership was and is limited to the king and princes of England as well as a very few knights of distinguished service. The insignia of the Royal Order is a blue garter, and because of this, blue ribbons have come to be a reward for any supreme achievement.

POLITICS & HISTORY

Why are political positions referred to as "left" and "right"?

Over two hundred years ago, King Louis XVI of France was forced to convene a form of parliament for the first time in more than a century. At the assembly, the more radical delegates took up seats on the left of the King, while their conservative counterparts sat on his right. Ever since, liberal views have been referred to as from the left, and conservative ideas as from the right.

Why are those seeking political favour from elected officials said to be "lobbying"?

The term *lobbying* originates from the earliest days of the British Parliament, where an extensive corridor runs between the Chamber of Lords and the House of Commons. Because the general public were allowed into this corridor, or lobby, it was where constituents waited to meet with their representatives in order to influence their votes on current legislation. This practice was called "lobbying" because it took place in the lobby.

Why do we say that a political candidate on a speaking tour is "on the stump"?

When early European settlers were moving west and clearing the land, every farm had an abundance of tree stumps in their fields. "Barnstorming" politicians who looked for a place of prominence to be seen and heard by the gathered electorate would invariably find a large tree stump to stand on from which he would make his pitch. This gave us the expression "on the stump," which is still used to describe a politician seeking election.

Why are some politicians called "lame ducks"?

A *lame duck* is a powerless American politician. After an election in a parliamentary system, such as that found in Britain or Canada, the House reconvenes and the winners immediately form the new government. In the American system, however, the newly elected congress doesn't take control for months, leaving those who have lost still in charge. During this time, because they can't pass anything meaningful, the powerless politicians are as useless as lame ducks.

Where did the phrase *spin doctor* come from?

The term *spin doctor* first appeared in the *New York Times* during Ronald Reagan's campaign for re-election in 1984. "Spin" is the twist given a baseball by a pitcher throwing a curveball to deceive the batter, while a "doctor" is someone who fixes a problem. Therefore, a "spin doctor" is someone who, faced with a political problem, solves it by putting a twist on the information to bend the story to his or her own advantage.

What does it mean when someone suffers a "sea change"?

Sea change is a term often used in politics that refers to a surprising and significant change from a previous position. Because early sailors were familiar with the sudden and unpredictable temperament of the sea, one minute calm and life-threatening and dangerous the next, they introduced the expression "sea change" into everyday English language meaning any sudden transformation.

Why do we say that healing a relationship is "mending fences"?

In 1880, the strong-willed senator John Sherman was testing the water for a presidential nomination. He slipped out of Washington but was followed to his Ohio farm by a reporter who found the senator talking with a high-ranking party official while standing near a fence. When the reporter asked what they were doing, the response, "We're mending fences," gave him his headline, and it became a new phrase for healing relationships.

Within a democracy, what are the fourth and fifth estates?

Within British history, the first three estates with influence over legislation were the Church, the House of Lords, and the House of Commons. The term *fourth estate* has meant different forces of influence over Parliament at different times, including the army. It was first used to describe the press during a debate in the House of Commons in 1828 and has retained that meaning ever since. The *fifth estate* was added to include radio and television.

Why when someone tells a secret do we say he's "spilled the beans"?

As a system of voting, the ancient Greeks placed beans in a jar. They called these small beans or balls "ballota," which gives us the word *ballot*. A white bean was a "yes" and a brown bean was a "no." The beans were then counted in secret so the candidates wouldn't know who voted for or against them. If the container was knocked over, and the beans were spilled, the secret was out of the jar.

Why did Abraham Lincoln's son withdraw from politics?

In 1865, Robert Lincoln rushed to his father's deathbed. Sixteen years later, as Garfield's secretary of war, he was with that president when he was shot by an assassin. In 1901, Robert arrived in Buffalo for the American Exposition just in time to see President McKinley murdered. After that, Robert Lincoln vowed never again to be in the presence of an American president.

Why do monarchs refer to themselves using the "royal we"?

When Roman consuls spoke of public issues they did so on behalf of all those with whom they shared power and so they used the plural pronoun *we*, instead of the singular *I*. The first king to use the "royal we" was Richard I, implying that he was speaking for his subjects as well as himself. It's improper for non-royals to use the plural self-reference, so when Margaret Thatcher did it in 1989, we were not amused.

How did Edward VII make it fashionable to leave the bottom button of a man's vest undone?

King Edward VII had a large appetite and an even larger tummy. He began leaving the bottom button of his vest undone because after a meal he simply couldn't do it up. Those who didn't want to make the king uncomfortable did the same, and so it became the fashion of the day. Edward's bulging belly may in part have been a consequence of his favourite dish, which was, of course, chicken à la king.

Why is the Irish gift of the gab called "blarney"?

Kissing the Blarney Stone at Blarney Castle near Cork, Ireland, is supposed to transfer the gift of gab to the kisser, but the idea that the word *blarney* meant a smooth talker came from the mouth of Elizabeth I of England in 1602. She had insisted that Dermot McCarthy surrender Blarney Castle as proof of his loyalty, but he kept coming up with excuses — so many excuses, in fact, that the Queen once exclaimed in exasperation, "Odds Bodkins, more Blarney talk!"

Why is some extreme behaviour called "beyond the pale"?

The expression dates back to the English Crown's first efforts to control the Irish by outlawing their language and customs. But the unruly Irish were just that, and by the fifteenth century the English still controlled only a small area around Dublin, protected by a fortification called "The Pale," meaning sharp sticks (i.e., impaled). To the British, to go "beyond The Pale" meant that you were entering the uncivilized realm of the wild Irish.

Where did the expression "paying through the nose" come from?

In Northern Ireland during the ninth century, the British introduced a harsh poll tax of one ounce of gold per year on all Irish households. The tax was nicknamed the "Nose Tax" because if a person didn't or couldn't pay, he had his nose slit. This cruel but effective procedure gave rise to the expression "paying through the nose," meaning if unreasonable due payments aren't made, there will be dire consequences.

Why is someone displaying absolute loyalty said to be "true blue"?

With the slogan "a true covenantor wears true blue," the Scottish Presbyterians adopted blue as their colour in the seventeenth century during their defense of their faith against Charles I. The instruction came from Numbers 15:38 in the scriptures, which tells the children of Israel to fringe the borders of their garments in ribbons of blue. Blue is a powerful symbol of Judaism and the national colour of Israel.

Why do we say "justice is blind"?

The Egyptian pharaohs, concerned that courtroom theatrics might influence the administration of justice, established the practice of holding trials in darkened chambers with absolutely no light. That way, the judge wouldn't be moved by anything but the facts. It's this principle that inspired *Lady Justice*, the well-known statue of a woman in a blindfold holding the scales of justice that is often found outside contemporary courtrooms.

Why do we say a graduating lawyer has "passed the bar"?

To control rowdiness, a wooden bar was built across early courtrooms to separate the judge, lawyers, and other principle players from the riffraff seated in the public area. That bar, first used in the sixteenth century, also underlies the English word *barrister*, the lawyer who argues the case in court. When someone has "passed the bar" or has been "called to the bar," it means he or she is now allowed into the closed-off area.

Why, when someone has been fooled, do we say he's had "the wool pulled over his eyes"?

In British courts, both judges and attorneys wear wool wigs, a custom that originated in the eighteenth century. The judge's wig is larger than the lawyer's, so he's often called the "bigwig." When a crafty lawyer wins at trial against all odds, it's as though the lawyer had blinded the judge with his own wig. It's said he just had "the wool pulled over his eyes."

Why do we say that someone caught in a dishonest or criminal act "got nailed?"

In the early days of criminal justice, punishment was often barbaric. Public hangings and floggings were commonplace, and for lesser crimes, the infliction of public humiliation and pain on the criminal was considered necessary to deter others from committing similar crimes. One such deterrent was to nail the convicted person's ears to the hangman's scaffold, where he or she would spend the day as a public spectacle. They had been "nailed."

Why were executions held at sunrise?

In prehistoric times, executions of condemned prisoners were carried out as sacrificial ceremonies to the rising sun. In the Middle Ages, because the executions were public, they continued to be held early in the day so as not to attract huge crowds. It wasn't until well into the twentieth century that more enlightened societies brought capital punishment indoors, not because executions were shocking, but because they were too popular.

What is the origin of the phrase, "I'll be hanged if I do and hanged if I don't"?

When America was fighting for its independence, the British poet Thelwall was arrested after enraging King George with his liberal, seditious support for the colonies. In prison he wrote to his lawyer, "I shall be hanged of I don't plead my own case," to which his lawyer replied, "You'll be hanged if you do!" His lawyer got him off, and the phrase became a slogan that contributed to the demise of the royal cause in America.

Why do we refer to an important issue as "the burning question" of the day?

During a time when the church and the state were equal in government, anyone failing to follow the state religion was burned at the stake. Those who demanded the separation of church and state were considered heretics, and thousands who were caught discussing the issue were burned at the stake. Because of this, whenever there was a secret debate on religious freedom, the subject was referred to as "the burning question."

Why when someone is betrayed do we say he was "sold down the river"?

After 1808 it was illegal for deep southerners to import slaves, and so they were brought down the Mississippi River from the North to the slave markets of Natchez and New Orleans. This gave the northerners a way of selling off their difficult or troublesome slaves to the harsher plantation owners on the southern Mississippi, and it meant that those selected or betrayed would be torn from their homes and families to be "sold down the river."

Why, when there's no turning back, do we say, "The die is cast"?

When you say, "The die is cast," you are quoting Julius Caesar. In 49 BC, the Roman general stood and thought long before crossing the Rubicon River into Italy with his army, a move that would break Roman law and start a civil war. When he made his decision and moved forward, he said, "Alea jacta est" (the die is cast), meaning, as when throwing dice, that the outcome is in the hands of fate, and there is no turning back from the consequences. Another phrase with a similar meaning came out of this same event: *Crossing the Rubicon* means taking a step or action that sets you on an irrevocable path.

WAR & MILITARY

Why when someone dies do we say, "He bought the farm?"

During the Second World War, airmen introduced the term "he bought the farm" after a pilot was shot down. The expression caught on with all the armed services and meant that if you gave your life for your country, your impoverished family would receive insurance money for your death, which would help pay off the mortgage on the family farm. Death for your country meant you were "buying the farm" for your parents.

Why is a glaring error called a "snafu"?

During the Second World War, massive military operations were so huge they were usually fouled up by their sheer weight and size. The frustrated servicemen called them SNAFUs, an acronym for "Situation Normal: All Fouled Up." Some say that "fouled up" was a polite adaptation for family use, but regardless, the expression *snafu* lived on, and now, as it did then, means a glaring error.

Why is a restricted limit called a "deadline"?

A deadline is an absolute limit, usually a time limit, and was popularized by the newspaper business, in which getting stories written and printed on time is of ultimate importance. But the expression comes from American Civil War prisoners, who were kept within crude makeshift boundaries, often just a line scratched in the dirt or an easily breached rail fence. They were told, "If you cross this line, you are dead," and soon the guards and prisoners simply called it what it was: a deadline.

Why do paratroopers shout "Geronimo" when they jump from a plane?

During the Second World War, Native American paratroopers began the custom of shouting the name of the great Indian chief

Geronimo when jumping from a plane because, according to legend, when cornered at a cliff's edge by U.S. cavalrymen, Geronimo, in defiance, screamed his own name as he leaped to certain death, only to escape both injury and the bluecoats.

Why when someone ignores the rules do we say he "turned a blind eye"?

In 1801, while second in command of a British fleet near Copenhagen, Horatio Nelson was told that his commander had sent up flags ordering a retreat. Nelson lifted his spyglass to his previously blinded eye and said he couldn't see the order, and then he ordered and led a successful attack. Nelson's insubordination became legend and gave us the expression "turn a blind eye."

Why do we say, "I heard it through the grapevine"?

During the American Civil War, a Colonel Bee set up a crude telegraph line between Placerville and Virginia City by stringing wires from trees. The wires hung in loops like wild grapevines, and so the system was called the "Grapevine Telegraph," or simply "the grapevine." By the time war news came through the wires it was often outdated, misleading, or false, and the expression "I heard it through the grapevine" soon came to describe any information obtained through gossip or rumour that was likely unreliable.

Where did croissants, or crescent rolls, originate?

In 1683, during a time when all the nations of Europe were at war with each other, the Turkish army laid siege to the city of Vienna. The following year Poland joined Vienna against the Turks, who were ultimately forced to lift the siege in 1689. As a celebration of victory, a Viennese baker introduced crescent-shaped rolls, or "croissants," copying the shape of the crescent Islamic symbol on the Turkish flag.

During the American War of Independence, which country contributed the most soldiers to fight alongside the British?

The country that contributed the most soldiers to fight with the British against Washington was America itself. By 1779, there were more Americans fighting alongside the British than with the colonists. Washington had about thirty-five hundred troops, but because one-third of the American population opposed the revolution, up to eight thousand loyalists either moved to Canada or joined the British Army.

What exactly is a last-ditch stand?

In the sixteenth century, when an army attacked a walled city or fortress, they would advance by digging a series of trenches for protection until they were close enough to storm the walls. If there was a successful counter-attack, the invaders would retreat by attempting to hold each trench in the reverse order from which they had advanced until they might find themselves fighting from the "last ditch." If they failed to hold that one, the battle was lost.

Where did the expression "the whole nine yards" come from?

During the South Pacific action of the Second World War, American fighter planes' machine guns were armed on the ground with .50 calibre ammunition belts that measured exactly twenty-seven feet, or nine yards, in length before being loaded into the fuselage. If, during mortal combat, a pilot gave everything he had by firing all his ammunition at a single target, it was said he'd given it "the whole nine yards."

What is the origin of the twenty-one gun salute?

All salutes are signals of voluntary submission. Early warriors simply placed their weapons on the ground, but when guns came along, the ritual of firing off or emptying cannons was done to illustrate to approaching foreign dignitaries that they had nothing to fear. In 1688, the Royal Navy regulated the number of guns to be used in saluting different ranks. For a prime minister, nineteen guns should be used, but for royalty or heads of state, the salute should be done with twenty-one guns.

In modern warfare, is it infantry or machines that determine the outcome?

Machines win modern wars. A 1947 study found that during the Second World War, only about 15 to 25 percent of the American infantry ever fired their rifles in combat. The rest, or three-quarters of them, simply carried their weapons, doing their best not to become casualties. The infantry's purpose is not to kill the enemy, but rather to advance on and then physically occupy his territory.

Why is an overly eager person or group said to be "gung-ho?"

The adjective *gung-ho* comes from the Chinese word *gonghe*, meaning "work together." It entered the English language through U.S. Marines who picked it up from the communists while in China during the Second World War. Because the marines admired the fervour of the Chinese leftists in fighting the Japanese, while the rightists under Chiang Kai-shek seldom fought, they adopted "gung-ho" as a slogan. They emulated the communists with "gung-ho" meetings and eventually called themselves "the gung-ho battalion."

Where did the word *assassin* come from?

While mounting a jihad against the invading Christian Crusaders in the 1300s, Hassan ben Sabah controlled his command of radical killers with a potion that gave them dreams of an eternity in a garden where young women pleased them to their heart's content. The potion was from hashish, and these young killers became known as hashish eaters, which in Arabic is *hashashin*, or as the Crusaders pronounced it, "assassin."

Why when two people share the cost of a date do we say they're "going Dutch"?

War has influenced the slurs in our language more than anything else. For example, when a soldier runs from battle the French say he's gone travelling "English style," while the English say he's on "French leave." During the Anglo-Dutch wars of the seventeenth century, British insults were that "Dutch courage" came from a bottle while a "Dutch treat" meant that everyone paid their own way, which of course was no treat at all.

Why do the military say "Roger" then "Wilco" to confirm a radio message?

During the Second World War, the U.S. Navy used a phonetic alphabet to clarify radio messages. It began, Alpha, Baker, Charlie, Dog, and went on to include Roger for "R." Because "R," or "Roger," is the first letter in *received*, it confirmed that the message was understood. On the other hand, "Wilco" is a standard military abbreviation for "will comply."

Why is the bugle call at day's end called "taps"?

In the seventeenth century, the British borrowed a Dutch army custom of sounding a drum and bugle to signal soldiers that it was time to stop socializing and return to their barracks for the night. The Dutch called it "taptoe," meaning "shut off the taps," and the abbreviated "taps" became a signal for tavern owners to turn off the spigots on their beer and wine casks. After lights out, taps signals that the soldiers are safely home, which is why it's played at funerals.

Why is a secret enemy amongst us referred to as a "fifth column"?

Any secret force within an enemy's midst during wartime is called a *fifth column*. The phrase comes from the Spanish Civil War, when the general leading the 1936 siege of Madrid with four columns of infantry was asked if four were enough. He replied that he had a fifth column hiding inside the city. Since then a *fifth column* has meant a secret organized force amongst the enemy or ourselves.

Why are those for and against war called "hawks" and "doves"?

Those who side with war have been called "hawks" since 1798, when Thomas Jefferson coined the term *war hawk*. The description of those who favour peace as *doves* is from the biblical book of Genesis. When Noah sent a dove over the water to see if it was receding, it returned with an olive leaf, indicating there was land nearby. The modern use began during the Cuban Missile Crisis and continues to the present.

What does the *D* stand for in *D-Day*?

Although *D-Day* has become synonymous with the Allied landing on June 6, 1944, in Normandy, it was used many times before and since. The *D* in *D-Day* simply stands for "day," just as the *H* in *H-Hour* stands for "hour." Both are commonly used codes for the fixed time when a military operation is scheduled to begin. "D minus thirty" means thirty days before a target date while "D plus fifteen" means fifteen days after.

Why, when someone we trusted turns against us, do we say he's "shown his true colours"?

Sailing under false colours means to sail under the enemy flag, and it was once a legitimate naval manoeuvre used to get close enough to the enemy for a surprise attack. At the last moment, just before opening fire, the false colours were lowered and replaced by the ship's "true colours." Although such deception is now considered dishonourable, we still say when someone we trusted reveals himself as the enemy that he is showing his "true colours."

Why do we call a traitor a "turncoat"?

Someone who changes sides during a war is called a "turncoat" because of the actions of a former duke of Saxony who found himself and his land uncomfortably situated directly in the middle of a war between the French and the Saxons. He quickly had a reversible coat made for himself, one side blue for the Saxons, and the other side white for the

French. Then, depending on who was occupying his land, he could wear the appropriate colour of allegiance.

Why when abandoning ship do we say "women and children first"?

In 1852, the HMS *Birkenhead* was off to war in South Africa when she ran aground and sank off the coast of the Cape. The only useable lifeboats were quickly filled by the 20 women and children on board, while the 476 soldiers lined up on deck to go down with the ship. This is where the tradition of "women and children first" was born, and in naval circles is still called "the Birkenhead drill."

Why is gossip called "scuttlebutt"?

The word *scuttlebutt* comes from sailors of the British Navy. Nineteenth-century warships had large wooden casks with holes cut in the lid for drinking water. The word *scuttle* means a hole, like the one created to scuttle a ship, or in this case, the one in the cask. The water cask itself was called a *butt*. And just as is done around the water coolers of today's offices, sailors exchanged the latest gossip while getting a drink at the scuttlebutt.

How did a crushing public humiliation become known as a "Roman holiday"?

The Etruscans of ancient Italy ritually honoured their dead war heroes by sacrificing the lives of all prisoners seized in battle. After conquering the Etruscans, the Romans borrowed and embellished the ritual by having the prisoners kill each other. They turned the slaughter into public gladiatorial games and declared the spectacle a Roman holiday, which became an expression synonymous with any cruel and crushing public destruction.

Why do we say, "It's cold enough to freeze the balls off a brass monkey"?

Early warships fired iron cannonballs from a stack piled next to the cannon. To keep them in place, they used a square piece of rust-proof brass with indentations to secure the bottom layer of balls. This plate was nicknamed the *monkey*. When it got cold enough, the mischievous brass monkey would shrink, causing the balls to fall out and roll all over the deck. It was "cold enough to freeze the balls off a brass monkey."

HOLIDAYS

Which culture began celebrating the new year with a feast of food and alcohol?

The earliest recorded New Year's festival was in ancient Babylon in what is now Iraq. Before the introduction of a calendar year, the celebration took place in spring during the planting season. The Babylonian feast was elaborate, lasting eleven days, and included copious drinking and eating in a tribute to the gods of fertility and agriculture. Celebrating the new year was both a thanksgiving and a plea for a successful new harvest.

What is the origin of New Year's resolutions?

In medieval times, during the last feast of the Christmas week, knights of the realm were required to place their hands on a peacock and vow to continue living up to their pledge of chivalry. This was known as the knight's "peacock vow." The New Year's custom of resolving to live a better life originated with the Babylonians, who promised the gods that they would return all borrowed farm and cooking tools and pay off personal debts.

How accurate is the Groundhog Day forecast?

In German folklore, if it's sunny when he emerges from hibernation, a groundhog will be frightened by his own shadow and return to his lair; therefore crops shouldn't be planted because there will be another six weeks of winter. In fact the groundhog comes out hungry and ready to mate, but if he's still dozy and his senses are dulled, he goes back to sleep. As a forecaster, the groundhog is accurate only 28 percent of the time — about the same as the weatherman.

How did Valentine become the patron saint of lovers?

In 270 AD, the mad Roman emperor Claudius II outlawed marriage because he believed married men made for bad soldiers. Ignoring the emperor, Bishop Valentine continued to marry young lovers in secret until his disobedience was discovered and he was sentenced to death. As legend has it, he fell in love with the jailer's blind daughter, and through a miracle he restored her sight. On his way to execution, he left her a farewell note ending in, "From Your Valentine."

How did March 17 become St. Patrick's Day?

When the time came to honour the patron saint of Ireland's birthday, church officials gathered solemnly to choose a day, then realized that most of St. Patrick's life was a mystery. They finally narrowed his birth-date down to either March 8 or 9, but because they couldn't agree which was correct, they decided to add the two together and declared March 17 to be St. Patrick's Day.

How did the shamrock become a symbol of St. Patrick?

In the fifth century, Patrick, the patron saint of Ireland, transformed that country from its pagan roots to Christianity. During an outdoor sermon, Patrick was struggling to explain the Holy Trinity when he spotted a shamrock. He used its three leaves to illustrate how the Father, Son, and Holy Ghost grew from a single stem, symbolizing one God sustaining the trinity, and ever since, the shamrock reminds the faithful of that lesson.

What are the origins of April Fool's Day?

Up until 1564, the French celebrated New Year's between March 25 and April 1, but with the introduction of the new Gregorian calendar the festival was moved to January 1. Those who resisted became the victims of pranks including invitations to nonexistent New Year's parties on April 1. Soon the April 1 celebration of a non-occasion became an annual festival of hoaxes.

How did the rabbit and eggs become symbols of Easter?

The word *Easter* comes from the ancient Norse word *Ostara*, which is what the Vikings called the festival of spring. The legend of a rabbit bringing Easter eggs is from German folklore, which tells of a poor woman who, during a famine, dyed some eggs then hid them in a chicken's nest as an Easter surprise for her children. Just as the children discovered the nest, a big rabbit leaped away, and the story spread that it had brought the eggs.

How did we start celebrating Mother's Day?

In 1907 Miss Anna Jarvis of West Virginia asked guests to wear a white carnation to the church service on the anniversary of her mother's death. But Mother's Day became increasingly commercial, and Miss Jarvis spent the rest of her life trying to restore its simplicity. The strain of her efforts to stop Mother's Day and what it had become led her to an insane asylum, where she died alone in 1948.

How did Father's Day get started?

During a Spokane, Washington, Mother's Day service in 1910, a Mrs. Sonora Dodd thought of how she and her five brothers had been raised on a small farm by her single father. She proposed a Father's Day celebration, but although it caught on locally, it was a political hot potato and didn't receive permanent recognition until an edict by President Richard Nixon in 1972. Father's Day is now the fifth-largest card-sending occasion in North America.

Why do children demand "trick or treat" during Halloween?

When the Irish introduced Halloween to America, children celebrated with a night of mild vandalism. Their bag of "tricks" included breaking or soaping windows or overturning outdoor toilets. Soon they realized that adults would offer candy or other "treats" to stop these tricks. They then offered the homeowner a choice of giving them goodies or suffering the consequences. This mild blackmail demand came as, "Trick or treat?"

Why do we carve jack-o'-lanterns for Halloween?

In Irish folklore, a supreme con man named Jack, or "Jack-o," once tricked the Devil himself. Upon his death, his sins barred him from heaven, and because he had once fooled the Devil he couldn't enter hell. After a lot of begging he finally persuaded Satan to give him one burning ember. Placed in a hollowed-out turnip it served as a lantern to light his way through the afterlife. Later in North America, the plentiful pumpkin replaced turnips for use as "Jack-o's lanterns."

Where did the customs of Halloween come from?

The ancient Celts celebrated October 31 as New Year's Eve. They called it "All Hallows Eve." They believed that on that night, all those who had died in the previous twelve months gathered to choose the body of a living person or animal to inhabit for the next year before they could pass into the afterlife. The original Halloween festival included human sacrifices and scary costumes, all designed to protect the living from the dead.

What was the original meaning of *merry* in "Merry Christmas"?

Today, *merry*, as in "Merry Christmas," suggests gaiety, a mood for celebration, but its original meaning was quite different. For example, the carol we sing as "God Rest Ye, Merry Gentlemen," should read "God Rest Ye Merry, Gentlemen." The word was at least four hundred years old when it was first written down in 1827, and at that time *merry* didn't mean joyous, but rather, peaceful or pleasant.

Was *Rudolph* the only name of the red-nosed reindeer?

In 1939, when Robert May, a copywriter for Montgomery Ward, wrote a promotional Christmas poem for that Chicago department store, its principal character was "Rollo" the Red-Nosed Reindeer, but the corporate executives didn't like that name, nor did they approve of May's second suggestion, "Reginald." It was May's four-year-old daughter who came up with "Rudolph," and the title for a Christmas classic.

How much would all the gifts cost in "The Twelve Days of Christmas"?

Because the golden rings are pheasants and not jewellery, the most expensive item in "The Twelve Days of Christmas" is seven swans a-swimming, at US$7,000, followed by ten lords a-leaping and nine ladies dancing. The current price of a partridge in a pear tree is $34, which is the hourly rate for eight maids a-milking. So when everything is added up, the tab is $15,944.20.

What were the bizarre ingredients of history's most exotic Christmas pies?

An early English saying was, "The devil himself dare not appear in Cornwall during Christmas for fear of being baked in a pie." Records show that living creatures from blackbirds to pheasants, from foxes to rabbits, and in one case even a dwarf, were cooked into Christmas pies at temperatures not hot enough to kill them. Then, as a festival highlight, the crust was broken, and the enclosed creatures would fly, hop, or run among the guests.

How much weight does the average person gain over Christmas?

In the Middle Ages, Christmas banquets started at three in the afternoon, with appetizers and fortified mulled wine followed by ten main courses, and lasted until midnight. Today, over the holidays, North Americans consume 24 million turkeys and 112 million cans of cranberries. We drink 108 million quarts of eggnog and 89 million gallons of liquor. The average weight gain over the Christmas holidays is four to six pounds.

What is the origin of Boxing Day?

Beginning in the Middle Ages, Boxing Day was known as St. Stephen's Day in honour of the first Christian martyr. Although unknown in the United States, Boxing Day is still observed in Britain, Canada, New Zealand, and Australia. It's called "Boxing Day" because on the day after Christmas, the well-off boxed up gifts to give to their servants and tradespeople, while the churches opened their charity boxes to the poor.

ANIMALS

Why do we call a predictable trial a "kangaroo court"?

The expression "kangaroo court" came out of Texas in the 1850s. It meant that the accused's guilt was predetermined and that the trial was a mere formality before punishment. *Kangaroo* was a Texas reference to Australia, a former British penal colony where everyone had been guilty of something, and so if a convict were accused of a new crime, there would be no doubt of his guilt.

When a person is upset, why do we say someone's "got his goat"?

When someone "gets your goat," it usually means you've lost your temper or become angry enough to be distracted. It's a term that came from a horse trainer's practice of putting a goat in a stall with a skittish racehorse to keep him calm before a big race. An opponent or gambler might arrange for the goat to be removed by a stable boy, which would upset the horse and its owner and so reduce their chances of winning.

Why is something useless and expensive called a "white elephant"?

The term "white elephant" comes from ancient Siam, where no one but the king could own a rare and sacred albino, or white, elephant without royal consent. The cost of keeping any elephant, white or otherwise, was tremendous, and so when the king found displeasure with someone he would make him a gift of a white elephant, and because the animal was sacred and couldn't be put to work, the cost of its upkeep would ruin its new owner.

Why do we call a leg injury a "charley horse"?

The phrase *charley horse* has its roots in baseball. At the beginning of the twentieth century, groundskeepers often used old and lame horses to pull the equipment used to keep the playing field in top condition. The Baltimore Orioles had a player named Charley Esper, who, after years of injuries, walked with pain. Because his limp reminded his teammates of the groundskeeper's lame horse, they called Esper "Charley Horse."

Why are there "bulls" and "bears" in the stock market?

An eighteenth-century proverb mocks the man who "sells the bearskin before catching the bear." A "bearskin speculator," like the man in the proverb, sold what he didn't yet own, hoping that the price would drop by the time he had to pay for it. "Bulls" speculate, hoping the price will rise. The analogies come from a time when fights were staged between the two animals, in which a bear needed to pull the bull down while the bull fought by lifting the bear with its horns.

How long is a furlong?

The furlong is an ancient British unit of measurement, literally meaning the length of a furrow. It's the distance a horse can pull a plow without resting, which was calculated at exactly 220 yards, or 201.168 metres. When the Romans introduced the mile to Britain, it was changed in length to accommodate a tidy eight furlongs. This was done because all property and other precise distances such as that of a horserace were measured locally in furlongs.

Why is an informer called a "stool pigeon"?

A "stool pigeon" is someone who betrays a group or cause to which he or she belongs. In their efforts to attract passenger pigeons, hunters would tie or nail a single pigeon to a stool and wait for a flock to be drawn to the cries of the desperate bird. Then, as they approached, the birds would be shot by the thousands. This practice continued until the species became totally extinct. The poor bird that unwillingly played the traitor was called a "stool pigeon."

Why do we say that someone with money is "well heeled"?

Before cockfighting was banned in 1849, individual birds were often fitted with sharp steel spurs, giving them an advantage in mortal combat. They were "well heeled." In the nineteenth century, the expression became slang for anyone armed with a weapon. Then, around 1880, the term began to mean anyone who was well-off financially and who could overcome any obstacle with money instead of a weapon.

Why is an innocent person who takes the blame for others called a "scapegoat"?

The term *scapegoat* or *escape goat* entered the English language with William Tyndale's translation of the Hebrew Bible in 1525. Under the Law of Moses, the Yom Kippur ritual of atonement involved two goats. One was sacrificed to the Lord, while all the sins of the people were transferred to the other. The scapegoat was then led into the wilderness, taking all the sins of the Israelites with it.

Why do we say that something worthless is "for the birds"?

In the days before automobiles, the streets were filled with horse-drawn carriages, and these animals quite naturally left behind deposits from their digestive systems. These emissions contained half-digested oats that attracted swarms of birds, which took nourishment from the deposits. The people of the time coined the expression *for the birds* as meaning anything of the same value as these horse-droppings.

Why is an unknown contestant called a "dark horse"?

Sam Flynn, a travelling Tennessee horse trader, often found a horse race planned in the same town as an auction. So he mixed a coal black racing stallion named Dusky Pete in with his workhorses, then quietly entered him in the local races and wagered heavily on Dusky Pete, who would invariably win. As word spread of Sam's deception, so did the caution: "Beware the dark horse."

Why do we call male felines "tomcats"?

A 1760 book titled *The Life and Adventures of a Cat* became so popular that from then on, all un-neutered male cats were called "Tom" after the book's feline hero. A female cat that has procreated is called a "queen," a title easily understood by any cat lover. Legend has it that one such cat lover, the great prophet Mohammed, once cut off the sleeve of his shirt before standing rather than disturb a sleeping kitten.

Why do we say, "Never look a gift horse in the mouth"?

It's considered rude to examine a gift for value, and the expression "Never look a gift horse in the mouth" means just that. The proverb has been traced to St. Jerome, who in 400 AD wrote a letter advising a disgruntled recipient of a gift of a horse to accept it in the spirit given without looking for flaws. It was then, and is still, common practice to look into a newly acquired horse's mouth, where you can tell its age by the condition of its teeth.

Why when astonished would someone say, "Well, I'll be a monkey's uncle"?

During the famous Scopes trial in 1925, a Tennessee schoolteacher, John T. Scopes, was accused of breaking that state's law by teaching

Darwin's theory of evolution rather than the Biblical origins of mankind. The trial was a sensation and astonished many who had never heard that humans might be related to the apes, and from this came the expression, "Well, I'll be a monkeys uncle."

Why when we have no choice at all do we say it's a "Hobson's choice?"

Thomas Hobson lived between 1544 and 1631 and was the owner of a livery stable in Cambridge, England. He was a very stubborn man whom Seinfeld might have called the "Livery Nazi" because, regardless of a customer's rank, he would rent out only the horse nearest the stable door. Hobson became famous for never renting horses out of order, so "Hobson's choice" came to mean, "take it or leave it."

How did pumpernickel bread get its name?

During the winter of 1812, while Napoleon's army was retreating from Russia, the only available food was stale, dark bread. Although his men were dying from hunger, Napoleon ensured that his great white horse, Nicholl, always had enough to eat, which caused the soldiers to grumble that although they were starving there was always enough "pain pour Nicholl," or "bread for Nicholl." When anglicized, "pain pour Nicholl" became "pumpernickel."

Why is misleading evidence called a "red herring"?

A "red herring" is a false clue leading detectives off the track during a criminal investigation. The term comes from a practice once used to train police dogs. When herring is smoked it becomes red, and when the young dogs were being trained to follow a scent, the trainers tossed smoked fish around to test their ability to follow a trail. Escaping prisoners learned of the practice and often took red herring along to distract the dogs sent after them.

Why is "until the cows come home" considered a long time?

If left to their own devices, cows in pasture will regularly show up at the barn for milking twice a day: once in the morning and once in the evening. The expression "'til the cows come home" first appeared in the sixteenth century when most people were familiar with the cycles of farm life. It was often used when a party went on long into the night — it would have to end in the morning when the cows came home and needed milking.

Why do we say that someone who has wasted his life has "gone to the dogs"?

In prehistoric China, for hygiene and safety reasons dogs weren't allowed inside the city walls. It was also forbidden to dispose of garbage within the city, and so the designated dump outside the walls was where the stray dogs found food. When undesirables and criminals were banished from the city and forced to compete with the dogs for food at the garbage dump, it was said they had "gone to the dogs."

Why do we say a hysterical woman is acting like she's "having kittens"?

In medieval times and during the American era of witch trials in Salem, whenever an unfortunate pregnant woman began to have premature pains or extreme discomfort, the authorities suspected that she had been bewitched. Because witchcraft and cats were synonymous, they feared that she was about to have a litter of kittens and that the creatures were scratching to get out from the inside. They would say her hysteria was because she was "having kittens."

Why do we use the word *wildcat* to describe a risky venture?

Whether it's a strike or an oil well, the word *wildcat* describes anything that is considered risky and has a good chance of failing. It comes from a time before regulations when state banks like the Bank of Michigan issued their own money. That bank's notes had a panther on the face and were called "wildcats." When the bank went down, so did a lot of fortunes. From then on, all high-risk ventures were described as wildcats.

Why do we call a computer problem a "bug"?

According to Grace Hopper, who led the team that developed the first large-scale computer for the American Navy in 1945, the word was coined when, after tracing an unexplained problem for days, they finally found the cause to be a two-inch bug, a moth, that had gotten stuck in the relay system. From then on, all unexplained computer problems were called bugs.

Why is do we say someone who is successful is "bringing home the bacon"?

This thousand-year-old expression came from a common British competition of trying to catch a greased pig at a country fair. But the first time it was recorded and entered into modern use in North America was in 1910, when, after her son won a championship fight, Jack Johnson's mother told the press, "My boy said he'd bring home the bacon." From then on, "bringing home the bacon" meant achieving success.

Why do we call money saved for a rainy day a "nest egg"?

The term *nest egg* usually refers to savings that compounds or grows with interest or through investments. The expression is an old one and comes from a trick poultry farmer's use to increase a hen's egg-laying ability. By placing a false egg (often a doorknob) in her nest, the farmer fools the chicken into laying more eggs than she otherwise would, meaning more money for the farmer, which he credits to his "nest egg."

How did we get the idea that the stork delivered babies?

The suggestion that storks delivered babies came from Scandinavia and was promoted by the writings of Hans Christian Andersen. Storks had a habit of nesting on warm chimneys and would often lift articles from clotheslines then stuff them into these nests, which to children looked like they were stuffing babies down the flue. The stork is also very nurturing and protective of its young, which helped it become symbolic of good parenthood.

Why do we say, "Every dog has his day"?

In ancient times, just as today in third-world societies, dogs lived miserable lives with little or no human care, which led to the hard-times expressions, "it's a dog's life," "sick as a dog," and "dog-tired." As for the proverb "Every dog has his day," it was first recorded as an epilogue after the famed Greek playwright Euripides was killed by a pack of dogs in 405 BC.

Why is taking the "hair of the dog" a hangover cure?

In the Middle Ages, people treated a dog bite with the ashes of the canine culprit's hair. The medical logic came from the Romans, who believed that the cure of any ailment, including a hangover, could be found in its cause. It's a principle applied in modern medicine with the use of vaccines for immunization. "The hair of the dog" treatment for hangovers advises that to feel better, you should take another drink of the same thing that made you feel so bad.

Why do we say when someone has a raspy voice that he has a "frog in his throat"?

The expression "frog in your throat" doesn't come from sounding like a frog because you have a cold or sore throat. It originates from an actual Middle Ages medical treatment for a throat infection. Doctors believed that if a live frog was placed head-first into a patient's mouth the animal would inhale the cause of the hoarseness into its own body. Thankfully, the practice is long gone, but the expression "frog in your throat" lives on.

What is the difference between a "flock" and a "gaggle" of geese?

Any group of birds, goats, or sheep can be referred to as a flock, but each feathered breed has its own proper title. Hawks travel in *casts*, while it's a *bevy* of quail, a *host* of sparrows, and a *covey* of partridges. Swans move in *herds*, and peacocks in *musters*, while a flock of herons is called a *siege*. A group of geese is properly called a *gaggle*, but only when they're on the ground. In the air they are a *skein*.

BELIEFS & SUPERSTITIONS

Why is a horseshoe thought to be good luck?

A horseshoe's charm comes from the legend of Saint Dunstan, who, because of his talent as a blacksmith, was asked by the Devil to shoe his cloven hoof. Saint Dunstan agreed, but in carrying out the task, he caused the Devil such pain that he was able to make him promise never to enter a house that has a horseshoe hanging above the doorway. Thus, from the Middle Ages on, the horseshoe has been considered good luck.

Why does breaking a wishbone determine good luck?

Twenty-four hundred years ago, because roosters heralded the sunrise and hens squawked before laying an egg, the Etruscans thought they were soothsayers. Because the sacred fowl's collarbone resembled a human groin, it was believed to have special powers and was called a wishbone. The Romans introduced the custom of two people pulling on the wishbone to see whom luck favoured. The winner was said to have gotten "a lucky break."

Why is the ladybug considered good luck?

Called either "ladybird" or "ladybug," the little red beetle with the black spots is the well-known and beloved subject of a nursery rhyme and is called a "lady" after the Virgin Mary because it emerges around March 25, the time of the Feast of the Annunciation, which is also known as Lady Day. Called the "Mary bug" in German, the ladybug brings good luck to a garden by eating unwanted pests.

Why is Friday the thirteenth considered to be bad luck?

The number thirteen represents Judas, the thirteenth to arrive at the Last Supper. Friday by itself is unlucky because it was the day of Christ's Crucifixion. Years ago, the British set out to disprove these superstitions. They named a new vessel HMS *Friday*, laid her keel on a Friday, and then sent her to sea on a Friday that fell on the thirteenth. The plan backfired: neither ship nor crew was ever heard from again. Then, of course, there's *Apollo 13*.

Why is it considered bad luck to walk under a ladder?

This superstition comes from the idea that many early cultures considered a triangle to be a sacred symbol of life. For Christians, a triangle represents the Holy Trinity. A ladder against a wall forms a triangle with the ground, and so to walk beneath it would be to disrupt a sanctified space and risk divine wrath. Even earlier, Christians considered the ladder resting against a wall to represent the ladder that rested against the cross during the Crucifixion, and therefore evil. For this reason condemned criminals were forced to walk under the gallows ladder — the entranceway to eternal darkness. The executioner always walked around it to position the noose.

How did spilling salt become a symbol of bad luck?

As man's first food seasoning, and later a food preservative and a medicine, salt has been a precious commodity for ten thousand years, so spilling it was costly as well as bad luck. This superstition was enhanced by Leonardo da Vinci's painting of the Last Supper, within which Judas has spilled the table salt as a foreboding of tragedy. Because good spirits sat on the right shoulder and evil on the left, tossing spilled salt over the left shoulder became an antidote.

Why do we cross our fingers when wishing for luck?

Crossing our fingers for luck predates Christianity and originally involved two people. In the pagan ritual, a close friend placed his or her index finger over the index finger of the person making the wish in order to help trap the wish at the centre of a perfect cross, which is where benevolent spirits lived. To ensure the wish stayed in place and on the wisher's mind, it was often tied to the finger with string, a practice that eventually evolved into a memory aid.

Why do we say "Bless you" after a sneeze?

The ancient Greeks believed a blessing might prevent evil from entering your body during its unguarded state while you sneeze. Our tradition comes from the black plague of 1665, when sneezing was believed to be one of the first symptoms of the disease. Infection meant certain death, and so the symptom was greeted with the prayer, "God bless you," which through time has been shortened to "Bless you!"

Why do we call sadness "the blues"?

The blues were around long before African Americans put them to music. The expression originates in the belief of early English settlers that "blue devils," or mean spirits, had followed them to their new land. These devils were thought to be the cause of sadness, and so a bout of depression was called "the blues." Because no one could have been sadder than the black slaves, their raw expression of the mood in a unique and brilliant musical form became known as "the blues."

What is Tecumseh's Curse?

The great Shawnee Chief Tecumseh, who died fighting with Canada against the United States' invasion in the War of 1812, placed a curse on the American presidency. He proclaimed that every president elected in a year that ends in a zero would die during his term. Since then, every president elected in such a year has died in office, with the exception of Ronald Reagan, who was shot, but survived. Here is a complete list of presidents affected by the curse:

- William Henry Harrison, elected in 1840, died of pneumonia one month into his presidency.
- Abraham Lincoln, elected in 1860, was assassinated in 1865 at the beginning of his second term.
- James A. Garfield, elected in 1880, was assassinated in 1881.
- William McKinley, elected for his second term in 1900, was assassinated in 1901.
- Warren G. Harding, elected in 1920, died of Ptomaine poisoning in 1923.

- Franklin D. Roosevelt, elected for his third term in 1940, died of a cerebral hemorrhage in 1945 at the beginning of his fourth term.
- John F. Kennedy, elected in 1960, was assassinated in 1963.
- Ronald Reagan, elected in 1980, survived an assassination attempt while in office. Some say that by surviving he broke the curse.

Why are new ships christened with champagne?

Beginning around the tenth century with the idea that the departed spirits would guide seamen on the ocean, ships were christened, or blessed, with the blood of sacrificial victims, which was splashed throughout the vessel. Eventually those who thought this too barbaric began using red wine, but the Christian church complained that this was an affront to its sacraments, and so ships were christened with white wine, the best of which is champagne.

Why after boasting do we knock on wood?

When children play tag and hold a tree for safety, they are acting out a four-thousand-year-old custom of the North American Indians who believed that because the oak was most frequently struck by lightning, it was the home of the sky god. The Greeks came to this same conclusion two thousand years later and because both cultures believed that bragging or boasting offended that god, they knocked on the tree either to divert him from their bragging or to seek forgiveness.

Why do people in mourning wear black?

Today, mourners wear black as a symbol of sadness and respect for their lost loved ones, but it didn't start out that way. Many years ago it was believed that the spirit of the departed, fearing harsh judgement, would try to remain on earth by inhabiting a familiar body. The mourners wore black and stayed indoors or in shadows to hide from the departed spirit who sought to possess them.

Why are cemeteries filled with tombstones?

Today, a tombstone is a tribute marking someone's final resting place, but the custom began within ancient fears that the departed spirit might rise from the grave to search out and inhabit the body of a living person. To prevent this, the coffin was nailed shut, a heavy stone was placed on its lid, and it was buried deep in the ground. For even greater security, another heavier stone was placed on the surface over the grave, giving us the tombstone.

WORDS

Why do we call a dollar a "buck"?

The Indians taught the first European settlers the value of a buck. Like gold, deer or buckskin was used in trading as a unit of value against which everything else was assessed. "The buck stops here" is a different matter. That expression came from frontier poker, in which the buck was a knife made of buckhorn that was passed around the table to indicate who was dealing. When a hand was finished, the dealer "passed the buck" to the next player.

Why is a severe snowstorm called a "blizzard"?

The word *blizzard* didn't mean a snowstorm until 1870, when a newspaper editor in Estherville, Iowa, needed a word to describe a fierce spring storm. The word *blizzard* had been hanging around with no particular origin for about fifty years and was used to describe a vicious physical attack, either with fists or guns. After its use by the editor, what better word to describe a violent snowstorm than *blizzard*?

Why do we call luxurious living a "posh" existence?

In the days of their empire, British tourists travelled by ship from England to the warmer climates of India and the Mediterranean. Wealthy passengers on these voyages demanded cabins shaded from the sun, which meant being on the port side on the way out and the starboard side on the way home. Tickets for these cabins were marked "POSH," which stood for Portside Out, Starboard Home, and *posh* stuck as a word that signified luxury.

Why do we use the word *glitch* to define an unknown computer problem?

Along with space exploration came new expressions that are now everyday language. Astronauts said "affirmative" for yes, "check" to confirm a completed task, and "copy" to indicate that an instruction was understood. "Glitch," an unexplained computer malfunction, was first used to describe the Mercury space capsule's frustrating tendency to signal an emergency when none existed.

Why are the sides of a boat called "starboard" and "port side"?

In the primitive days of navigation, the helmsman stood at the stern of the ship, controlling the vessel's direction by hand with a rudder, which was on the right side and called a steer board, or as the Anglo-Saxons called it, a "starboard." The left side of the ship is called the "port" side, because with the steering mechanism on the right it was the only side that could be brought to rest against a harbour or port.

Why do we call the first weeks of marriage a "honeymoon"?

The custom of a "honeymoon" began over four thousand years ago in Babylon, when for a full lunar month after the wedding, the bride's father would supply his son-in-law with all the honey-beer he could drink. It was called the "honey month." The word *honeymoon* didn't enter our language until 1546, and because few people could afford a vacation, a honeymoon didn't mean a trip away from home until the middle of the nineteenth century.

Why do we say someone diverted from a goal has been "sidetracked"?

Early railroads had only a single track between destinations. Problems arose when a train was met by another going in the opposite direction or was about to be overtaken by a faster one. This dilemma was solved with the creation of sidings, short lengths of track built parallel to the main line where one train could pull over while the other went by. The train had been "sidetracked," meaning that, for a time at least, it wasn't going anywhere.

Why do we say someone charming has "personality"?

In the Greek and Roman theatres, actors wore masks to indicate the different characters they were playing. The Latin word for mask, *persona*, came to mean a personality other than that of the actor. Today, *persona*, or *personality*, still refers to the mask a person wears to hide his or her true character while playing a role for the outside world.

How did the dandelion and the daisy get their names?

The dandelion and the daisy are both named for a particular physical characteristic. The English daisy, with its small yellow centre and white- or rose-coloured rays, closes at night and reopens with daylight

like the human eye, and so it was named the "day's eye." The dandelion, because of its sharp, edible leaves, was named by the French "dent
de lion," the "tooth of a lion."

Why are Levi denims called "jeans"?

In the 1850s, when Levi Strauss ran out of tent canvas for the pants he
was selling to California gold miners, he imported a tough material from
Nimes in France called serge de Nim. Americanized, "de Nim" became
"denim." The word *jeans* is from the French word for Genoa, where the
tough cloth was invented. Jeans became popular with teenagers after
James Dean wore them in the movie *Rebel Without a Cause*.

Why are construction cranes and the mechanisms used for drilling oil called "derricks"?

The derrick, an instrument used for heavy lifting, got its name from a
famous London hangman. In the early 1600s, Godfrey Derrick built a
sturdy gallows from which he would execute some three thousand souls
by hanging. Because items hung and swayed from the cranes used to
load ships, longshoremen called them "derricks" after the executioner's
infamous device.

How did the word *curfew* come to mean "stay in your homes"?

The word *curfew* comes from the French *couvre-feu*, which means
"cover-fire" and was brought to England by William the Conqueror.
The original Curfew Law minimized the tremendous risk of fire by
ordaining that a bell be rung at eight o'clock each evening, signalling
everyone to either extinguish or cover their home fires. During political unrest, the same curfew bell signalled the public to clear the streets
and stay in their homes for the night.

What is the meaning of the word *factoid*?

Norman Mailer introduced the word *factoid* in his 1973 book *Marilyn*. He invented it by combining the word *fact* with *-oid*, a scientific suffix that means "resembling but not identical to." In other words, it's something that looks like a fact, but isn't. Factoids are built from rumours and used by irresponsible journalists to create a story when none exists.

Why is the word *mayday* used as an aviation distress call?

The distress call "mayday" comes from the French, who were leading pioneers in flight. In 1911 there were 433 licenced aviators in France, compared to just 171 in Britain and even fewer in the United States. Flying was a risky business, and it wasn't until parachutes and radios were introduced that the French call "M'aidez," or "help me," became Anglicized to the modern international distress call, "Mayday!"

Why is a surplus of anything called a "backlog"?

While a backlog of work might be a burden, it's better than no work at all, and in business it guarantees survival. Before stoves, or even matches, the kitchen fireplace was kept burning around the clock. This was done by placing a huge log, or back log, behind the fire that would keep smoldering once the flames had died down during the night. The embers from the back log could then ignite a new fire in the morning.

Why is the paved runway of an airport called a "Tarmac"?

The hard pavement surface we now call asphalt was discovered by chance when an Englishman named E. Purnell Hooley accidentally spilled tar onto some crushed stone. Hooley named this new black pavement by taking the last name of Scotsman John MacAdam, who had developed the use of crushed stone for a firm, dry highway, and pre-fixing it with "tar." *Tarmacadam* was a mouthful, however, and was soon shortened to *Tarmac*. Hooley patented Tarmac in 1903.

Why do we call a reaction of coercion and punishment a "boycott"?

The word *boycott*, meaning to ostracize an oppressor, originated in Ireland in the late nineteenth century. As punishment for falling behind in rent, poor tenant farmers in County Mayo were being tossed from their homes by Captain Charles Boycott, who was acting as the agent of an absentee English landlord. The tenants eventually forced Boycott's downfall by refusing to take in the harvest, making the repossessed land useless to its English owner.

Why do we call a quarter "two bits"?

European settlers brought their money with them to America, and coins made of precious metal were accepted everywhere at face value. The Spanish peso was divided into eight silver coins, which the English called bits, or pieces of eight. Two bits was one-quarter of a Spanish dollar. When money was printed and minted in the new world, although a dollar's coinage was divided by ten, the expression "two bits" continued to mean one-quarter of a dollar.

Why is a select roast of beef called a "sirloin"?

Legend has it that in 1617, during dinner and after a few goblets of wine, King James I of England suddenly stood and drew his sword and, laying it across the entrée, declared: "Gentlemen, as fond as I am of all of you, yet I have a still greater favourite — the loin of a good beef. Therefore, good beef roast, I knight thee Sir Loin and proclaim that a double loin be known as a baron."

Why is listening in on a private conversation called "eavesdropping"?

In medieval times, houses didn't have roof gutters to carry off rainwater; instead they had "eaves," which are the lower wide projecting edges of a sloping roof. These eaves protected the mud walls from damage from the rain dropping from the roof. If, during a sudden shower, someone sought cover by standing under an eave, they could hear everything that the people inside were saying. They were "eavesdropping."

Why is a large, controlled fire called a "bonfire"?

On June 24, or St. John's Day, early Britons lit chains of huge fires to support the diminishing sun. These fires were fed with the clean bones of dead farm animals and were called "bone fires," which evolved into *bonfires*. There were bone fires, wood fires, and a mixture of both wood and bones was called a "St. John's fire," a name given, naturally, to the fires that burned heretics at the stake.

Why is natural ability called "talent?"

In the ancient world a *talent* was a unit of weight used to value gold and silver. Today's use of the word comes from the Book of Matthew, wherein three servants are given equal amounts of money, or talent, by their master. Two invest wisely and profit while the third buries his and doesn't. That parable is how *talent* came to refer to the natural gifts we are all born with. The moral of the tale is that we must use our talents wisely or we will fail.

Why is socializing called "hobnobbing"?

When the Normans conquered England, they introduced the open hearth for cooking and heating. At each corner of the hearth was a large container for heating liquids. It was called a "hob." Near the fire was a table where the hob was placed for convenient serving. They called this table a "nob." When friends gathered by the warmth of the fire, they drank warm beer from the hob, which was served on the nob, and so they called it "hobnobbing."

Why are notes taken at a business meeting called "minutes"?

The reason the written records of a meeting are called the minutes is because, in order to keep up, the minute-taker wrote in a shorthand or abbreviation. The word used to describe this condensed writing was *minute* (my-noot), meaning "small," and because the spelling is the same, the minutes (my-noots) became *minutes*. The same circumstances apply to Frederick Chopin's Minute Waltz: It's really his small or minute (my-noot) waltz.

Why is extortion money called "blackmail"?

If there is "blackmail" then there must be "white mail." *Mail* was a Scottish word for rent or tax, and during the reign of James I, taxes or mail were paid in silver, which, because of its colour, was called "white mail." During the sixteenth and seventeenth centuries, bandits along the Scottish border demanded protection money from the farmers. Because black signified evil, this cruel extortion was called a black tax, or "blackmail."

Why after a foolish error do we call someone a "laughingstock"?

In early English, a *stock* was a tree trunk, and by the fourteenth century it figuratively meant the family tree or the consequences of breeding. For example someone might be from "farming stock" or "good stock," while an animal's breeding line was traced through their "livestock." If someone calls you a laughingstock, they are insulting your family tree as being one filled with fools from which you are the current crop.

Why are dining rooms called "restaurants"?

Up until 1765, diners were offered only what innkeepers chose to serve. But then, a Paris chef named Boulanger began offering a choice of nourishing soups to passersby and on a board hanging over the door he painted the word "Restaurant," meaning "to restore." Boulanger was so successful that throughout the world dining rooms still display his original sign, "Restaurant," a promise to restore energy.

Why do we call a large timepiece a "clock"?

Like *cloche* in French, *clock* literally means bell. When the large mechanical clock was invented in the fourteenth century it didn't tell time with a face and hands, but rather by sounding bells on the hour and eventually the quarter- and half-hour. This time device was named a *clock* because it told time by sounding bells. O'clock, as in twelve o'clock or five o'clock, is an abbreviation for "of the clock," or "of the bells."

Why, when we don't understand someone, do we say they're talking "gibberish"?

An eleventh-century alchemist translated into Latin the original eighth-century writings of an Arabian alchemist named Jabir. If his work had been discovered he would have been put to death, and so he wrote Jabir's formulas in a mystical jargon of his own creation. To anyone other than the author, the Jabir translations didn't make sense. And so anything like it was "Jabirish," which eventually became *gibberish*.

Why do we call the perfect world "Utopia"?

The word *Utopia* was created by the English philosopher Sir Thomas More in 1516 and was the title of his book that compared the state of life in Europe at the time with an imaginary ideal society. *Utopia* is from Greek meaning *nowhere*. The thrust of More's message was that an ideal world, or Utopia, will never exist, and that our only choice is to improve the standards of our existing society.

Why is noisy chaos referred to as "bedlam"?

The word *bedlam* is a medieval slang pronunciation of "Bethlehem," and its use to describe a mad uproar dates back to a London hospital for the insane. St. Mary in Bethlehem was incorporated in 1547 as the Royal Foundation for Lunatics. Because people could hear but only imagine the chaos inside, they began referring to any noisy, out-of-control situation as like that in "Bedlam" — Bethlehem hospital.

Why do we call a bad dream a "nightmare"?

There are different degrees of frightening dreams, but the most terrifying cause sensations of suffocation and paralysis. Literature best describes the sleeper's sensation in the stories of Dracula, but there was also a common female demon known as "the night hag." *Mare* is an Old English term for *demon* and comes from the same root as *murder*; therefore the demon, or mare, who visits at night was called a "nightmare."

Why is a disappointing purchase or investment called a "lemon"?

In 1910, the rotating slot machine appeared as a device for dispensing chewing gum and gave us the symbols still used on slot machines today. The spinning flavours were cherry, orange, and plum. Each wheel had a bar reading "1910 Fruit Gum," and three of those in a row paid off in a jackpot of gum. But, also like today, if any row came up a lemon there was no payout at all, which gave us the disappointed expression, "It's a lemon."

Why is a ten-dollar bill called a "sawbuck"?

Among the many slang expressions for denominations *deuce*, originally a mild curse of the devil when the numbe up in dice or cards, and the Yiddish *fin* for a five. *Sawb_____ ___ ten comes from the frame of a sawbuck, or sawhorse, on which farmers held logs to be cut into firewood. This frame rested on two X-shaped supports that resembled the two roman numerals for ten found on the early American ten-dollar bill.

Why does *criss-cross* mean back and forth?

Schoolchildren in the sixteenth century worked lessons on a thin wooden board that hung from their belts. On it were printed the alphabet, the numbers, and the Lord's Prayer. Because it was preceded by a Maltese cross the alphabet was called the Christ-cross-row. Students reciting from the board always began with the prayer, "Christ's cross be my speed." Two centuries later, Christ's cross had become "criss-cross."

Why are the secondary consequences of a greater event called the "aftermath"?

The chain of events set in motion by a major occurrence is often called an *aftermath*. *Math* is from an old English word meaning "to mow." The second, smaller crop of hay that sometimes springs up after a field has been mowed is called the *aftermath*, or "after mowing," and although it is next to useless, it is a problem that has to be dealt with for the good of the fields.

Why is a concise promotion called a "blurb"?

The word *blurb*, meaning an inspired recommendation, comes from an evening in 1907 during an annual trade dinner of New York publishers

.ere it was customary to distribute copies of new books with special promotional jackets. For his book, humorist Gelett Burgess caused a sensation with a cover drawing of a very attractive and buxom young woman whom he named "Miss Belinda Blurb." From then on, any flamboyant endorsement would be known as a *blurb*.

EXPRESSIONS

Why do we call a good meal a "square" meal?

In the eighteenth century, a British sailor's sparse diet consisted of a breakfast and lunch of little more than mouldy bread and water. If he were lucky, the third meal of the day included meat and was served on a square tin platter. Because of the shape of that platter, they called it their "square" meal: the only substantial meal of the day. Three squares now means three good meals a day.

Why do we call midday the "noon hour"?

The "noon hour" has shifted several times throughout history, and at one time, when Christians prayed twice a day, it meant both midday and midnight. In the original Old English the noon hour was the hour for prayers, which at the time was the ninth hour of daylight, or three o'clock in the afternoon. The singular prayer time, or noon hour, changed to midday, or twelve o'clock, during the Middle Ages in Britain.

Why do we say "Goodnight, sleep tight"?

Sometime during the sixteenth century, British farmers moved from sleeping on the ground to sleeping in beds. These beds were little more than straw-filled mattress tied to wooden frames with ropes. To secure the mattress before sleeping, you pulled on the ropes to tighten them, and that's when they began saying, "Goodnight, sleep tight."

Why do we say "We're just gonna hang out?"

"Hanging out" usually means getting together for no particular reason other than to pass time and see what's happening. The expression comes from a time before commercial signs, when English shopkeepers set up poles in front of their stores from which they would hang flags describing their goods. These flags were called hangouts, and they became a place where people would stop to linger and gossip with their friends.

Why is mealtime sometimes called "chow time"?

Chow is a Mandarin Chinese word meaning to cook or fry, while in Cantonese, chow means food. The chow chow is a breed of dog that was in fact originally bred by the Chinese to be eaten. In the early days of North American settlement, Chinese immigrants, because of their culinary talents, were often put to work cooking for the labour gangs who then picked up the phrase "chow time" as meaning it's time to eat.

Why is something in great shape said to be in "A1 condition"?

In their early days, Lloyd's of London used an "A list" to classify sailing ships for insurance purposes. Only vessels meeting strict specifications would go to the top of that list, where they were said to be in A1 condition. When, as a general insurer, the company began covering everything from Mary Hart's legs to Jennifer Lopez's derrière, Lloyd's continued to classify anything first rate as "A1."

When someone loses his job, why do we say he "got the sack"?

"Getting the sack" has come to mean getting fired or dismissed from anything, including a love affair. The expression entered the language long before the industrial era, at a time when workers carried their tools from job to job in a sack. When the job was done, or the labourer was discharged, the boss or employer would simply hand the worker his tool sack. He was literally "given the sack."

Why when dreaming of better times do we say, "When my ship comes in"?

During the nineteenth century, Bristol, England, was the busiest seaport in the world, and while local sailors were at sea, tradesmen would extend credit to their wives until the very day their husband's ship returned to port. Because the ship meant her family's livelihood, women referred to their husband's vessel as "my ship," and when asking for credit would promise to pay the tab "when my ship comes in."

Why do we say a corrupt person has "gone to the Devil"?

In Victorian times, to "go to The Devil" was to visit a bar on Flat Street near the London Civil Courts. The Devil was a favourite pub for lawyers, who seemed to spend more time in that bar than in their offices. If a client thought his money had "gone to The Devil" to pay for his lawyer's drinks, he might visit the legal offices to ask for an explanation, where he would be told that the absent lawyer had indeed "gone to The Devil."

Why do we say, "I'll be there with bells on"?

During the frontier days, peddlers travelling between settlements had to move as silently as possible through the hostile forest, but when they approached a homestead or town they would take out their muffled bells and hang them on their horses' necks to announce their arrival. The peddlers' arrival "with bells on" brought news, letters, and goods from the outside world, and was an exciting event for the isolated settlers.

Why do wives call money from their husbands "pin money"?

Pin money became an English phrase to describe extra cash set aside by wives to run the household at the turn of the twentieth century, when pins were rare enough to be sold on just two days of the year, January 1 and 2. Although through time pins became more commonplace and far less expensive, the British courts still enforce any prenuptial agreement or property lien demanded by the wife as the "pin money charge."

Why is a special day called a "red letter day"?

In the Middle Ages, simple survival meant working long and hard from sunrise to sunset, so any break, such as for a religious festival, was a very special day. Called "holy days," these feasts were marked on the calendar in red, giving us the expression "red letter day." Around the fifteenth century, "holy days" became "holidays," meaning simply a day off work, still marked on the calendar in red.

Why, when getting serious, do we say, "Let's get down to brass tacks"?

In the days of the general store, cloth came in bulk and was sold by the yard. The storekeeper, who quickly became expert at measuring, often used the length of his arm as a measure of each yard being purchased. If the measurement was challenged, the seller would remeasure the cloth against two brass tacks embedded in the counter that were precisely a yard apart. The issue was therefore settled by getting down to those two brass tacks.

Why, if someone isn't up to the job, do we say he isn't "worth his salt"?

Thousands of years ago, before money was introduced, workers and soldiers were often paid with a negotiated quantity of salt. More than as a seasoning, salt's value was in its use as a preservative or cure for meat, as well as a medicine. The early Romans called this payment a "salarium," which gave us the word *salary*. If a man wasn't worth his salt, he wasn't worth his salary.

Why is something recently manufactured called "brand new"?

The original meaning of the word *brand* was a fire burning within a furnace or forge. To say an item, whether pottery or forged metal, was "brand new" meant it was fresh from the fires of its creation. This usage dates back to the sixteenth century. The verb *to brand* comes from the same source and means to mark ownership on something, from wine casks to livestock, using a hot iron from a fire.

Why do we say that someone intoxicated is "three sheets to the wind"?

Sailing ships are controlled with an intricate system of ropes, called "halyards," "lines," and "sheets," whose function it is to move or hold things in place. Sheets are the ropes that control the sails. If one is loose, the sails will flap in the wind. Two loose sheets will affect the ship's steadiness. "Three sheets to the wind" and the vessel will reel off course like a drunken sailor.

Why is a pirate ship's flag called a "Jolly Roger"?

The purpose of a pirate ship's flag was to signal a merchant vessel that if it didn't surrender, it would be boarded and plundered by force.

Pirates used a variety of flags. One was an hourglass that signalled time was running out. The skull and crossbones is of course the most famous flag, and it got its name "Jolly Roger" from the English pronunciation of "Ali Rajah," which is Arabic for "king of the sea."

Why are hot summer days called "the dog days"?

Sirius, the "dog star," is within the constellation Canis Major and is the brightest in the heavens. The ancient Egyptians noted that the dog star's arrival in July coincided with the annual flooding of the Nile, which was important for a good harvest. The Romans believed that, because of its brightness, the dog star Sirius added to the heat of the summer sun, and so they called July and August "the dog days."

Why is a misleading sales pitch called a "song and dance"?

During the days of travelling vaudeville shows, there were featured stars, and there were fillers. The fillers were the comics who were hired to keep the audience amused by telling jokes within a song and dance routine until the next headliner was ready to come on stage. Since then, any well-rehearsed routine that is intended to divert your attention from what you came to see has been called a "song and dance."

Why do we say that a bad deal will only "Rob Peter to pay Paul"?

In the mid-1700s the ancient London Cathedral of St. Paul's was falling apart, and the strain on the treasury was so great that it was decided that it would merge with the diocese of the newer St. Peter's Cathedral in order to absorb and use their funds to repair the crumbling St. Paul's. The parishioners of St. Peter's resented this and came up with the rallying cry, they're "robbing Peter to pay Paul."

Why when someone is snubbed do we say they're getting "the cold shoulder"?

In Europe during the Middle Ages, the "cold shoulder" had two purposes. If guests overstayed their welcome they were often served cooked but cold beef shoulder at every meal until they tired of the bland diet and left. The other "cold shoulder" was leftover mutton that was saved to give to the poor to discourage them from begging at the pantry.

Why do we tell someone to "get off his keister" when we mean stand up and do something?"

The word *keister* is derived from *kiste*, the German Yiddish word for strongbox or suitcase. Early Jewish immigrants who arrived with all their belongings in a kiste would often sit on them while waiting to be processed through customs, and the English-speaking agents didn't realize that it was the suitcase and not their bottoms they were referring to when they told the immigrants to "get off their keisters."

Why when someone takes credit for another person's achievement do we say she "stole his thunder"?

In the early 1700s, English playwright John Dennis introduced a metallic device that imitated the sound of thunder. The production it was created for failed, and the thunder device was forgotten until months later, when, while attending another play at the same theatre, Dennis heard the unmistakable sound of his invention. He made such a public fuss that all of London picked up the phrase, they've "stolen my thunder."

Why, when something is stopped cold, do we say somebody "put the kibosh" on it?

To "put the kibosh" on something is an Irish expression meaning to put an end to it. The word *kibosh* is Gaelic and means "cap of death." It was, in fact, the black skullcap donned by a judge before he sentenced a prisoner to death. In modern usage it means, as it did to the condemned, "Your path of destruction has ended."

Why do we say "by hook or by crook" when determined to accomplish something by any means?

"By hook or by crook" means by fair means or foul. Today a *crook* is a thief who uses deception, and to *hook* something means to steal it. That particular definition comes from the thirteenth century, when hooks used for shepherding were also used by peasants to bend branches when stealing firewood or fruit from the royal forest, and since their deceit was called "crooked" after the shape of their hooks, these thieves became known as *crooks*.

Why is a stash of surplus money called a "slush fund"?

The term *slush* began as a sailors' reference to the grease from the cook's galley, which was used to lubricate the ships masts. When the voyage was over, the surplus grease was sold, and the money was put into a "slush fund" to be shared by the enlisted men. By 1839, when a ship returned to port, any surplus supplies or battle-damaged equipment was also sold and the money added to the profits from the grease in the slush fund.

Why do we say we're "boning up" when studying or preparing for an examination?

The phrase *boning up* comes from a British teacher of Greek and Latin who wanted to make life easier for his students. With that goal in mind he translated the Greek and Latin classics into English and then had them published and distributed within his classroom. His name was Mr. Bohn, and his grateful students called this new, speedier method of studying the classics "Bohning up."

Why is cheating on corporate accounting ledgers called "cooking the books"?

If someone is using creative accounting, he is usually breaking the law, and so he needs someone with sophisticated bookkeeping skills comparable to those of a skilled chef who can prepare a dish so artfully that no one can tell how it was done. If authorities discover that the books have been cooked and criminal charges are laid, it is said that the accountant and the employer have "cooked their own goose."

What do we mean when we say someone's from the "wrong side of the tracks"?

In the nineteenth century, railway tracks usually ran right through the centre of town, and it was the prevailing winds that determined which was the right or wrong side to live on. As the town developed, the wealthy built homes on the cleaner, windward side of the tracks, while industrial development and the working class were confined to the other, dirtier side. To be from the "wrong side of the tracks" meant you were from a poor or working-class family.

Why do we say "either fish or cut bait" when we mean "make up your mind"?

There are two main jobs on a fishing boat. One is to "cut bait," which means to prepare or cut "junk" fish for a hook, or for "chum," which is dumped in the water to attract other fish. The second job is to do the actual fishing. So the admonition "Either fish or cut bait" doesn't mean either fish or cut your line; it means make up your mind and decide which job you're going to do, and just do it.

What are we doing when we "gild the lily"?

To *gild* something is to cover it with a thin layer of gold. Because a lily is already in a state of natural perfection, gilding it would only be excessive. The expression is a misquote from Shakespeare's *King John*, during which the king's barons describe his second redundant coronation, "As throwing perfume on the violet or to gild refined gold to paint on the Lily."

What do we mean by the "sixth sense"?

Humans are credited with five senses: sight, hearing, touch, taste, and smell. So someone with a "sixth sense" is gifted with an unexplained perception outside of the common five. The expression *sixth sense* comes from a study of blind people reported in 1903 in which it was found that, although deprived of sight, some of the subjects could perceive or sense certain objects in a room in a way that defied scientific understanding.

Why, when something doesn't make sense, do we say "it's neither rhyme nor reason"?

When you say that something is "neither rhyme nor reason," you are quoting Sir Thomas More. After reading something a friend had written, Sir Thomas told him that he would have to rewrite it in order to make his point clear. After his friend reworked the manuscript, More read it again, and this time he approved, commenting: "That's better, it's rhyme now anyway. Before it was neither rhyme nor reason."

Why do we say, "Put a sock in it" when we want someone to shut up?

The admonition, "Put a sock in it," meaning keep quiet, comes from the time of the earliest wind-up phonographs in which the sound

emerged from a horn. These early acoustic record players didn't have electronic controls or any muting device to raise or lower the volume, and so the only way to soften its sound was to stuff something into the horn. A sock was the perfect size, and so to lower the volume they would "put a sock in it."

Why is going to bed called "hitting the hay"?

When going to sea, early sailors had to provide for their own bedding. This need was catered to by merchants on the docks who, for a shilling, sold the seamen crude canvas sacks stuffed with hay. When heading off to sleep, a sailor would announce that he was going to "hit the hay." Although less crude than those coarse canvases, early North American settlers also used hay to stuff mattresses and pillows, so when going to bed, they too would "hit the hay."

Why when it appears that we can proceed with no danger do we say, "The coast is clear"?

The person who says, "The coast is clear," sounds as though he or she is being cautious about avoiding legal detection, and so it should. It originated as the standard cry from the man in the crow's nest of every pirate ship before it chanced a landing. When the captain verified with his telescope that there was no danger in going ashore, he would repeat the cry, "The coast is clear!" And so it became an order for his fellow smugglers to prepare to land.

Why when suggesting an exhaustive search do we say, "Leave no stone unturned"?

The advice to "leave no stone unturned" comes from Greek mythology, wherein the Oracle of Delphi, through his communication with the gods, had acquired great wisdom. Euripides wrote that when the oracle was consulted about how to find a defeated general's hidden treasure, he advised that the only way was "to leave no stone unturned." The expression and the advice have been with us ever since.

What is the origin of the phrase "tabloid journalism"?

On March 4, 1884, a British drug company registered the word *tabloid* for a very small tablet it was marketing. About the same time, large broadsheet newspapers were challenged by small-format journals, and because *tabloid* had come to mean anything small, that's what the new papers were called. These tabloids often resorted to gossip instead of hard news, which gave sloppy reporting the name "tabloid journalism."

Why is a rough interrogation called "the third degree"?

The *third degree* is a very difficult and sometimes brutal questioning, especially by police. In fact, without its sinister connotation, the expression comes from the Masonic Lodge and its three degrees of membership, each requiring an increasingly difficult examination. The first is Entered Apprentice, the second is Fellowcraft, and the third degree, the one most difficult to pass, is Master Mason.

Why do the phrases "dressed to the nines" and "putting on the dog" mean very well dressed?

The expression "putting on the dog," meaning showing off, comes from the practice leisurely wealthy women had of carrying lapdogs to afternoon social functions. "Dressed to the nines" comes from a time when the seats furthest from the stage cost one pence, and the closest, nine pence. Sitting in the expensive seats required dressing up to fit in with the well-off. It was called "dressing to the nines."

Why do we say that someone on target is "on the beam"?

Early aviators had a system of radio signals to guide pilots through fog and bad weather. Dots and dashes were beamed out from a landing field and picked up in the pilot's earphones. If he heard dot-dashes, he was too far left, and dash-dots meant he was too far right. But when the signals converged into a continuous buzzing sound, the pilot was "on the beam," or safely on course.

Why is someone lost if he "doesn't have a clue"?

The original spelling of *clue* was C-L-E-W, and its forgotten meaning is a "ball of yarn or string." A clew of string was unravelled as a guide out after entering an unfamiliar maze or a cave. If you became lost, all you had to do was follow the string back to the point of origin. In the modern cliché, if someone "doesn't have a clue," he is in the dark with no idea how to get out of his dilemma.

Why is a limited space called "close quarters"?

Being at "close quarters," meaning to be overwhelmed within a small space, is a naval term from the 1700s. Merchant sailing ships laden with valuable cargo had their decks outfitted with four strong wooden barriers with musket holes to which they could retreat and continue to fight if they were boarded by pirates or privateers. They referred to these desperate circumstances as fighting at "close quarters."

When someone survives disaster, why do we say he's "cheated the devil"?

The first recorded instance of "cheating the devil" can be found in the Hebrew Talmud. The devil offered a farmer two years of a flourishing harvest with the condition that the devil would get the crops grown underground for the first year, and those grown above the ground the following year. During the devil's below-the-soil year, the farmer grew wheat and barley. In the above-the-soil year he grew carrots and turnips, and thereby cheated the devil.

Why is going beyond the known limits called "pushing the envelope"?

"Pushing the envelope" is an aviation expression that refers to how test pilots received instructions to challenge the known limits of flight. These instructions, if not a death sentence, were very often a flirtation with disaster. The gravity of issuing such an order was understood but not spoken. Instead, the impersonal assignment came within an envelope, silently slid or pushed across a desk from one man to another.

Where did the insult "couldn't hold a candle" come from?

The derogatory expression "couldn't hold a candle" is from the sixteenth century. Before electricity, experienced workers needing light to work by would have a young apprentice hold a candle so that they could see to complete a complex job. Holding a candle for a skilled tradesman gave the apprentice a chance to watch and learn, but if he couldn't even do that properly, it was said disparagingly that "he couldn't hold a candle" to the tradesman.

Why do we say that someone looking for trouble has a "chip on his shoulder"?

In early England, one man would challenge another to a duel by slapping his face with a glove. The challenge was a serious matter of honour, and if the slapped man did not accept it, he would be branded a coward. Having a chip on your shoulder was kind of an early Wild

West equivalent of the glove slap, though generally less mortal in nature. Boys and men would place a woodchip on their shoulder, challenging anyone who dared knock it off to a fistfight. So, if a man had a "chip on his shoulder," he was clearly in an aggressive mood and spoiling for a fight.

Why is it said that something with proven quality has passed the "acid test"?

If someone has passed the "acid test," it usually means that he has proven his value through experience or trial. When gold was in wide circulation, jewellers and assayers needed a method of testing golden objects and nuggets that were brought to them for cash. Because nitric acid dissolves base metals but not gold, a drop was applied to the suspect object, and if the metal didn't dissolve, it had passed the acid test and was confirmed to be gold.

Why do we say a nervous person waits with "bated breath"?

The body has instinctive reactions to emotional circumstances, and one of these is how we breathe during times of apprehension. Our breathing becomes short and controlled when we are in crisis. *Bated* is a variation of the word *abated*, both meaning restricted. Therefore, when someone is in a state of fear or suspense and his breathing becomes restricted, he is said to be waiting with "bated breath."

Why do we say, "If you believe that, I've got a bridge I'd like to sell you"?

After the Brooklyn Bridge was built in 1883, a young con man named George Parker approached the gullible as its owner, and after explaining the fortune to be made through toll booths, he would sell the bridge for as much as fifty thousand dollars. Parker went to jail for life, but not before selling the Statue of Liberty, Grant's Tomb, and Madison Square Garden — and leaving us the expression, "I've got a bridge I'd like to sell you."

Why do we say that a victim of his own scheming has been "hoisted on his own petard"?

The phrase "hoisted with his own petard" is found in Shakespeare's *Hamlet*. It has come to mean that someone has been or will be hurt by the very device he's created to injure someone else. *Hoist* means to raise something into the air, while *petard* is an antiquated word for *bomb*. Therefore, if you were "hoisted on your own petard," it means you were blown up by your own bomb.

TRIVIA

How do statues of men on horses tell how the rider died?

Statues of horse and rider are exclusively of monarchs or great warriors and are usually found in places of honour. The tradition is that if the horse is depicted with all four hooves on the ground, the rider died of natural causes. If one hoof is raised, the rider's death came later from wounds incurred during battle, and if two hooves are in the air, the rider portrayed in the statue died on the battlefield.

What do the distress letters *SOS* stand for?

Morse code is a series of electrical impulses that signify the letters of a structured message. SOS doesn't stand for "save our ship" or "save our souls," as has been commonly believed. In fact, it stands for nothing. It was chosen as a distress signal at an international conference in 1906 because, at nine keystrokes — three dots, three dashes, three dots — it was thought to be the easiest combination to transmit.

What is the shortest English sentence ever created using all the letters of the alphabet?

Western Union developed the sentence, "The quick brown fox jumps over the lazy dog" as a test for their telex operators, and it's thirty-five letters long. However it isn't the shortest English sentence ever created using all the letters of the alphabet. That honour belongs to the sentence, "Jackdaws love my big sphinx of quartz," which was authored by an anonymous scholar and is just thirty-one letters long.

Why are there sixty seconds in a minute and sixty minutes in an hour?

Around 2400 BC, the ancient Sumarians, who used six as their mathematical base, divided a circle into 360 degrees, with each degree subdivided into another 60 parts, and so on. The Romans called these units *minute prima*, or first small part, and *secunda minuta*, or second small part. This system was perfect for round clock faces, and that's why we use minutes and seconds as divisions of time.

What is the world's largest number?

In order to calculate massive quantities, American Edward Kasner coined the "googol," which is a one followed by one hundred zeros. But the "googoplex" is now the largest number and is a one followed by a billion zeros, which allows us to calculate that the number of electrons passing through a forty-watt light bulb in a minute roughly equals the number of drops of water flowing over Niagara Falls in a century.

What English words rhyme with *orange, purple,* and *silver*?

In the English language, there are only two words that end in "GRY": *angry* and *hungry*. There are only three that end in "CEED": *exceed, proceed,* and *succeed,* while *liquefy, putrefy, rarefy,* and *stupefy* are the only four words ending in "EFY." As for *orange, purple,* and *silver,* poets and songwriters should stay away from them, because there are no words in the entire English language that rhyme with them — absolutely none!

If a coin is tossed and lands tails ten times in a row, what are the odds that it will be heads on the eleventh try?

After a coin has been tossed and landed tails ten times in a row, many amateur gamblers would be inclined to bet that the "law of averages" would favour the coin landing heads on the eleventh try. The problem is, the law of averages doesn't exist. The coin's probability of landing heads is still fifty-fifty — the same as on each previous toss.

Precisely who qualifies as a baby boomer?

A baby boomer is someone who was born after soldiers of the Second World War had come home and up to eighteen years later, so the period differs in some countries. In the U.S. and Canada, 20 million babies were born during the boom between 1946 and 1964. North America's first baby boomer, Kathleen Casey Wilkens, was born in Philadelphia one second after midnight on January 1, 1946.

Is Mount Everest the world's tallest mountain?

Mount Everest may be the world's highest mountain, but it's not the tallest. Hawaii's Mount Mauna Kea is four thousand feet taller, but its huge base is submerged, which means Everest rises higher above sea level. Actually, satellite measurements indicate that the Himalayan peak K2, at 29,030 feet, is two feet higher than Everest, but snow and erosion make precise measurements difficult to attain.

Was there ever a planet named Vulcan, as in the *Star Trek* series?

In 1845, scientists believed that the only explanation for Mercury's confusing and erratic orbit of the sun would be the presence of gravitational pull from an unseen nearby planet, which they named "Vulcan." Eventually Albert Einstein, through his theory of relativity, explained Mercury's behaviour, thus eliminating the hypothetical planet Vulcan — until it was resurrected by Gene Rodenberry in *Star Trek*.

Why do local telephone numbers never start with the number one?

The original dial telephone sent out a signal "click" for each number dialled. One click for 1, two "clicks" for 2, etcetera. The zero was reserved for the operator. "One" was never used because early switching systems read every signal as beginning with one click, regardless of the number you were dialling, and so technically, no phone number could start with 1. It continues today simply as tradition.

What is the origin of the Ivy League?

The term *Ivy League* has nothing to do with the ivy-covered walls of the prestigious schools to which it refers. Several Eastern U.S. schools — Harvard, Yale, Princeton, and Columbia — became known collectively as the "Interscholastic Four League," but the four was always written in Roman numerals — IV — and was pronounced "eye-vee." By the end of the Second World War, the league had expanded to include Brown, Cornell, Dartmouth, and the University of Pennsylvania. Although there were then eight schools included in the league, instead of changing its name, the league decided to spell it the way it had been traditionally pronounced, and so it became the "Ivy League."

Why is the lump in a man's throat called an Adam's apple?

The Adam's apple is found only in men, and it got its name from an ancient embellishment of the story of Adam and Eve. Folklore had it that when Adam swallowed the forbidden fruit, one large piece of the apple got stuck in his throat and remained there, forming a lump. This lump in every man's throat, his Adam's apple, is an eternal reminder of his humility in the eyes of God.

What is the difference between *bravery* and *courage*?

Both bravery and courage are acts of valour and imply a certain strength and fearlessness. There is, however, a subtle difference in meaning between the two words. *Courage* comes from the French word *coeur*, meaning heart. It is a quality of character that allows someone to carry through with a difficult premeditated plan of action. *Bravery*, on the other hand, comes from the Spanish word *bravado*, meaning a single or spontaneous act of valour. It is not planned, but rather a knee-jerk reaction that often occurs within a crisis.

Why are yards and metres so different in length?

In the twelfth century, Henry I of England decreed that a yard would be the distance from his nose to the thumb of his outstretched arm. As crude as this seems, Henry was only off by one-hundredth of an inch from today's version. The metre was introduced by the French after the revolution and was intended to be exactly one-ten-millionth the distance between the North Pole and the equator, which was incorrectly calculated as 39.37 inches.

Why did pirates wear earrings?

Earrings were used by seamen, especially warriors such as pirates, for very practical reasons and not for decoration. They were given to young sailors as a symbol of their first crossing of the equator, and their purpose was to protect the eardrums during battle. The pirates, especially those who fired the ships' cannons during closed combat with the enemy, dangled wads of wax from their earrings to use as earplugs.

If "possession is nine-tenths of the law," what are the points it outweighs?

The expression "possession is nine-tenths of the law" is from the eighteenth century and means that in the pursuit of justice possession in a dispute over property outweighs these nine other essential elements of a good court case: a lot of money, a lot of patience, a good cause, a good lawyer, good counsel, good witnesses, a good jury, a good judge, and good luck.

Why do we park on a driveway and drive on a parkway?

The words *parkway* and *driveway* come from the days when only the well-off could afford an automobile. The long, winding roads from the highway to the manor were, and are still, called "driveways." On the other hand, to ensure the pleasure of driving, highways were built carefully, with planted trees and groomed medians to imitate the natural beauty of a park, so they were called "parkways," meaning left in an enhanced natural state.

What was a "computer" before the electronic age?

The word *computer* first appeared in the seventeenth century as the job title of a person who did calculations as an occupation. Although slide rules were sometimes called computers, it wasn't until the 1940s, with the development of massive electronic data machines, that the human occupation of computing became obsolete. These mechanical devices became known as *computers*.

Is it the tower or the clock on the British Houses of Parliament that is called Big Ben?

"Big Ben" is neither the tower nor the clock of England's Houses of Parliament. Rather, it's the largest of the bells in the tower clock, which was installed in 1858. London newspapers of the time named it "Ben" after Sir Benjamin Hall, the commissioner of works who was responsible for adding the huge 13.5-ton bell to the tower.

Why are candies on sticks called lollypops?

At the end of the nineteenth century, most candies were too large and dangerous for a child's mouth, and because they were sold unwrapped, they inevitably caused a sticky mess on clothes, faces, and fingers. That was enough to make many parents keep their children from buying them. In a stroke of marketing genius, George Smith of Connecticut solved the problem by putting the candy on a stick. He named his invention after a famous racehorse of the time, Lolly Pop.

How did written punctuation originate?

It wasn't until the end of the fifteenth century that the Italian printer Aldus Manutius introduced the system of markings we call punctuation. The proper use of punctuation marks is a learned skill that has eluded even great writers ever since. Mark Twain once filled the last page of a manuscript with all the various symbols of punctuation and instructed his editor to disperse them within the story as he saw fit.

Why are BC, AD, BCE, and CE all used to give calendar dates to historic events?

In 525 AD the Christian church introduced a calendar using the year of Christ's birth, 1 AD, or "Anno Domini," as the starting point. Earlier events were BC, or "Before Christ." Uncomfortable with these references, non-Christians replaced BC with BCE for "Before the Common Era" and AD with CE, the "Common Era."

What do the words *algebra, sofa, sash,* and *sequin* have in common?

Algebra, sofa, sash, and *sequin* are among the hundreds of common English words that originated within the Arabic languages. A few others are: *magazine, alcohol, jar, cotton,* and *mattress. Racquet* comes from an Arabic word for *hand,* which is how tennis was originally played. The words *alcove, chemist, coffee,* and *chess* are also included among the everyday Arabic words that enrich our language.

Why are the abbreviations of pound and ounce, *lb.* and *oz.?*

The *lb.* abbreviation for *pound* comes from ancient Rome and is lifted from the Latin, "libra pondo," or "pound of weight." The *oz.* for *ounce* came from medieval Italy and is from *onza,* meaning a twelfth part, because at the time the English ounce was one-twelfth of the Roman pound of 330 grams. Although an ounce is now one-sixteenth of a pound, it's still abbreviated as *oz*.

Why is the speed of a ship measured in knots?

In the 1600s, sailors measured the speed of their sailing ships by tying knots in a rope at sixty-foot intervals, then further dividing and marking the space between the knots into ten equal parts that would each be one fathom in length. Then a heavy floating log was tied to the rope's end and thrown into the ocean. The rope was let out through a reel, and speed was measured by the number of knots that passed through the reel in thirty seconds of an hourglass.

What was the origin of a New York "ticker tape parade"?

Before the electronic age, ticker tape was a thin paper ribbon of information fed mechanically to the brokers on Wall Street. At day's end, floors were ankle deep with ticker tape. On October 28, 1886, the elaborate dedication of the Statue of Liberty was visible from the brokers' windows, causing such excitement that they began tossing ticker tape out the windows. That's how the ticker tape parade became a New York tradition.

Are the letters in the word *news* an acronym for north, east, west, and south?

Some early news sheets were headed with N-E-W-S as points of a compass, but it was simply a clever gimmick. The word *news* predates these publications and emerged with its current meaning within a letter written by King James of Scotland in 1423. In 1616, his descendant, James I of England, wrote another letter, which included the first recorded use of "No news is good news."

How did sunglasses originate?

In the thirteenth century, the Chinese invented dark glasses to be worn by judges so that none in the courtroom could read their eyes. The narrowly slit Eskimo goggles are prehistoric and are a protection against snow-blindness, not the direct sun. Modern sunglasses were a consequence of twentieth-century flight, designed by the American Army Air Corps in 1932 to keep the glare out of a pilot's eyes.